5 STEPS TO FINANCIAL FREEDOM

MONEY MANAGEMENT MADE EASY

JAMES D. WISE

D1451096

HENSLEY
PUBLISHING

Tulsa, OK

HENSLEY
PUBLISHING

ISBN 1-56322-084-9

FIVE STEPS TO FINANCIAL FREEDOM: MONEY MANAGEMENT MADE EASY

ABOUT PHOTOCOPYING

CONTENTS

INTRODUCTION   9

MONEY AND POSSESSIONS

1   Materialism   15

2   Ownership   29

3   Stewardship   41

FIVE STEPS TO FINANCIAL FREEDOM

4   Giving — Part 1   63

5   Giving — Part 2   81

6   Setting Goals — Part 1   105

7   Setting Goals — Part 2   117

8   Saving — Part 1   139

9   Saving — Part 2   151

10   Budgeting — Part 1   167

11   Budgeting — Part 2   183

12   Debt Reduction — Part 1   203

13   Debt Reduction — Part 2   223

IMPLEMENTATION

14   Application — Part 1   243

15   Application — Part 2   257

16   Application — Part 3   269

APPENDIX: PERSONAL TESTIMONY   281

NOTES   287

INTRODUCTION

All I ever wanted was to be rich. My career choice mattered little, so long as it would provide unlimited income potential. I was willing to work hard, as hard as necessary, so long as such work ensured the desired outcome: enough money to live in whatever house, drive whatever car, and buy whatever else I wanted. I had become convinced early in life that money was the only viable means of achieving true happiness. To me, success was clearly defined by what one had or didn't have; image, indeed, was everything.

Things didn't become complicated until I started to succeed. My first few goals were relatively easy to achieve: a new luxury car, a new home, a significant increase in my income. It actually seemed like I was having fun, at least until I noticed a most troubling pattern emerging. I would set my sights on some material goal and set a firm timetable for its acquisition. The challenge came, however, a few weeks *after* the goal had been achieved, when the thrill wore off and I was left with a renewed feeling of emptiness, not to mention another new monthly payment. When you earn a lot of money you can usually borrow enough to buy whatever you want. Such is the nature of our consumer-driven society. And I was all too willing to participate, motivated by a world full of material goods in need of an owner.

I've learned over the years that my attitude was not at all uncommon. As a non-Christian surrounded by other materialists, my drive for money and possessions seemed perfectly normal, even healthy. Surely *something* would eventually bring happiness and contentment. For those people not interested in spiritual matters it is only logical to assume that money is the solution to all of life's problems. In the absence of some standard of absolute truth by which to measure my attitudes and opinions, I naturally assumed that my beliefs about success were just as valid as anyone's. It was only when money and material possessions failed to provide the expected satisfaction that I began to question the entire process, wondering whether I had been deceived about what was truly important in life.

By the time I was in my early thirties I had acquired everything I ever thought I wanted. But rather than enjoying my so-called success, I was increasingly pressured and distraught. It wasn't working. I could honestly say at that point in my life that I was no happier than when I had begun my career and had nothing. It was this realization that led me on a wonderful journey that ended at the foot of the Cross. It was there, at the blood-stained feet of my Savior and Lord, that one life ended and a new one began (Galatians 2:20).

After coming to faith in Jesus Christ and spending considerable time studying what God's Word had to say about money and possessions, I naturally assumed that the rampant materialism in my former world was a problem pertaining only to non-Christians. I learned in time, however, that the lure of money and possessions is just as great a stumbling block for those inside the church. We still live in the flesh and the flesh is still sinful. Christians struggle just as mightily with materialism as do those outside the family of faith. That is my motivation for developing this study guide: to bring biblical truth to bear in the management of our financial resources. This will enable us to achieve a degree of freedom that is not possible apart from the application of these principles.

There are five specific groups of people for whom this study guide has been written. The first group is made up of those who are currently in financial crisis. Perhaps you, like me, have made every financial mistake imaginable. You have committed to this Bible study in desperation, hoping to find some means of immediate relief from the tremendous financial burden under which you have been living. If so, be encouraged. The answers you need are contained in the pages that follow. Be encouraged also that your loving Father stands committed to walking with you, and His mercy is infinitely greater than even the greatest financial trial.

The second group represents those who, though not yet in financial crisis, feel as though they are treading water, fighting to keep from slipping beneath the waves. You might be struggling each month just to make ends meet and you sense that you are one calamity away from financial disaster. You've tried everything you know to try but are still unable to get ahead. You, too, will be blessed as you work through this study. God has provided an abundance of information that you can begin applying to improve your financial circumstances significantly.

The third group is made up of folks who are doing well financially, but who somehow sense that they aren't consistently handling their finances in a way that is pleasing to God. Perhaps you've always had enough income to meet your needs and have never found it difficult to save and increase your resources. By any objective standard you are in good financial shape. Still, you sense that something is missing. It could be that you've never really considered God's perspective and you are ready to learn, or that you've been taught biblical financial principles but have never committed to applying them. In either case, this study should help you to quickly internalize the deep truths of Scripture and motivate you to begin experiencing the joy of living by them.

The fourth group might be the smallest, but they'll have the most fun with this study. I know because whenever I've had the privilege of teaching on this subject, several folks from this group are always present. If you are in this group, you have faithfully lived by biblical financial principles for many years. You've experienced financial freedom in the truest sense, having more than enough resources to meet all of your needs and giving away more than most of us could imagine. When social discourse turns to finances you can't hide the smile or the twinkle in your eye. You know intimately what God has to say about money, and you eagerly share His truth with all who will listen. Those in the first three groups no doubt wonder, as I used to when you attended my workshops, *Why in the world does this group need to go through a Bible study on finances?* The answer is as simple as it is delightful: It is because you love God's Word! You thrive on its application, and you derive great pleasure from reinforcing the principles you have so faithfully practiced. You have counseled numerous folks using these same principles, and you will probably be leading others through this study in the near future. If you are in this group, you were also on my mind as I wrote this study, and I pray that you will continue to bear fruit in your life and ministry.

The fifth group is not identifiable so much by their financial state as by their spiritual state. If you are in this group, you aren't quite sure about using the Bible as a guide for financial decision-making. Perhaps you get a bit uncomfortable when someone talks about Jesus, Christianity, or a personal relationship with God. You are interested in finances and you want to learn more about the subject, but a Bible study isn't at the top of your list of priorities.

If I've just described where you are, at least in part, then I will make a commitment to you before you begin. The principles taught in this book will transform your financial life. They are logical, practical, and true. The fact that they are grounded in God's Word notwithstanding, if you commit to completing this study purely for its financial content, you will not be disappointed. I thought of you while writing every chapter, and I've tried to honor your investment of time by providing a comprehensive financial process that will help you regardless of whether or not you accept the spiritual content. All I will ask of you is this: Study with an open mind. Where Bible passages are used, read them with a sincere desire to learn. If you are studying with a group, ask lots of questions. And when you have finished, please read the appendix and consider the claims of Jesus Christ. If you choose to reject this information, your financial life will still be greatly enhanced. If you choose to accept God's Word as truth, your life will be forever transformed, and you will know a freedom that cannot be expressed in words.

Whatever your particular reasons are for beginning this study, it is my fervent prayer that you will be rewarded. May the Lord richly bless your journey!

Money
and
Possessions

-1-
MATERIALISM

The devil led him up to a high place and showed him in an instant all the kingdoms of the world. And he said to him, "I will give you all their authority and splendor, for it has been given to me, and I can give it to anyone I want to. So if you worship me, it will all be yours."

—Satan, Luke 4:5-7

"Do not love the world or anything in the world. If anyone loves the world, the love of the Father is not in him. For everything in the world — the cravings of sinful man, the lust of his eyes and the boasting of what he has and does — comes not from the Father but from the world."

—John the Apostle, 1 John 2:15-16

Before we begin exploring the topic of materialism and considering the subtle ways in which it influences our view of money and possessions, let's take a simple test. You walk out to your mailbox tomorrow, and as you rifle through the stack of bills and junk mail you notice an envelope with no return address that appears to contain a check. Your hands begin to shake as you tear open the envelope and discover a check in the amount of $15,000 made out in your name. Your heart pounds as you read the cover letter. It is signed by an attorney and explains that this is your share of an inheritance from a deceased relative whose name you don't recognize.

Unsure as to whether this is legitimate, you call the toll-free number on the letterhead. First you talk to a receptionist, then an administrative assistant, and finally after several minutes of elevator music, you are speaking to the attorney who signed the letter. She quickly confirms that, in fact, you have a deceased relative who remembered you in his will. The $15,000 is yours, no strings attached. What will you do with it? Will you use part to pay down some consumer debt, or will you finally be able to afford some much-needed home repairs? Will you put it all in the bank in order to preserve it, or is there a dream vacation that you've always wanted to take but never could afford? Could this be your opportunity, finally, to drive a nicer car? Take a few moments to consider your present circumstances and, in the space below, write down exactly what you would do with this unexpected windfall, in order of priority. (Note: There are no "right" or "wrong" answers; only honest or dishonest ones!)

1. $_____ : _____
2. $_____ : _____
3. $_____ : _____
4. $_____ : _____
5. $_____ : _____
6. $_____ : _____

The choices you've made in the above exercise should provide some insight into your perspective about money. Most of us have financial tendencies that have been with us for years. These tendencies become increasingly apparent when we receive some unexpected funds, be it a tax refund, a gift from our parents, or an inheritance from a long-lost relative. As you go through this chapter, think about your financial priorities and consider whether they are in any way influenced by a materialistic worldview.

What exactly is *materialism*? Webster's defines it as "the tendency to be more concerned with material [things] than with spiritual goals or values."[1] As a former professional materialist, I hereby declare that this definition is much too tame. Materialism involves greed, covetousness, and the love of money. It results in our envying others who have what we don't have. It causes us to dwell on money and possessions and is characterized by an extreme lack of contentment. Materialism leads us to spend money we don't have, to buy things we don't need, to impress people we don't even like! Most of us have materialistic tendencies to some extent, whether or not we are willing to characterize them as such.

REFLECT
List several major purchases you have made recently.

_____

_____

_____

Which of these, if any, could you really not afford?

_____

_____

What do you think were your underlying motivations for these purchases?

_____

_____

_____

Since materialism presents itself in several ways and to varying degrees, we will look together at some of the symptoms of this fleshly disease, as well as some biblical insight into each.

Symptom 1: Love of Money

Many who suffer from this symptom may not even recognize their affliction. This habit is generally much more subtle than it appears, and it may manifest itself in several different ways. One indication of the love of money which afflicts those who have already accumulated some financial resources is an unhealthy obsession with the investment markets, including daily (or hourly) tracking of investment results and account balances. Rather than create and execute a prudent savings and investment plan, there is a tendency to constantly trade securities, frantically moving money from one investment to another in hopes of beating the market.

This symptom of materialism can be driven by either fear or greed, but the results are usually the same: many sleepless nights and wide mood swings. Capital gains lead to a great sense of victory and euphoria; investment losses bring intense despair. In between is a nervous preoccupation with daily events that may affect the financial markets. A great deal of time is spent combing the financial section of the newspaper and watching the stock market news on cable TV. At its worst, this symptom leads a person straight to the computer each evening for hours of gathering additional information via the Internet.

When caught in this trap, we usually justify our actions by quoting a few Bible verses on stewardship. We convince ourselves that it is our responsibility to gain as much information as we can in order to make wise investment decisions with the resources God has entrusted to our care. In reality, however, we have created an idol for ourselves, a golden calf to which we bow down and worship daily.

Most folks have learned by now that the majority of information available in the newspaper, investment newsletters, and financial press is either outdated or worthless. Scripture, on the other hand, lays out several timeless principles that are invaluable in managing investments:

1. DIVERSIFICATION: *Give portions to seven, yes to eight, for you do not know what disaster may come upon the land* (Ecclesiastes 11:2).

2. PROPER PLANNING: *The wisdom of the prudent is to give thought to their ways* (Proverbs 14:8); *a simple man believes anything, but a prudent man gives thought to his steps* (Proverbs 14:15); *the plans of the diligent lead to profit as surely as haste leads to poverty* (Proverbs 21:5).

3. SEEKING WISE COUNSEL: *Plans fail for lack of counsel, but with many advisers they succeed* (Proverbs 15:22); *whoever gives heed to instruction prospers, and blessed is he who trusts in the LORD* (Proverbs 16:20); *listen to advice and accept instruction, and in the end you will be wise* (Proverbs 19:20).

4. EXERCISING DISCIPLINE: *The proverbs of Solomon son of David, king of Israel: for attaining wisdom and discipline; for understanding words of insight; for acquiring a disciplined and prudent life* (Proverbs 1:1-3); *he who heeds discipline shows the way to life, but whoever ignores correction leads others astray* (Proverbs 10:17); *he who ignores discipline comes to poverty and shame, but whoever heeds correction is honored* (Proverbs 13:18).

5. NOT TRYING TO "GET RICH QUICK": *Dishonest money dwindles away, but he who gathers money little by little makes it grow* (Proverbs 13:11); *do not wear yourself out to get rich;*

have the wisdom to show restraint (Proverbs 23:4); a faithful man will be richly blessed, but one eager to get rich will not go unpunished (Proverbs 28:20).

Most or all of these instructions are ignored by the lover of money.

DISCOVER

Read Matthew 6:24-25. Which two "masters" are noted that we might choose to serve?

1. _____   2. _____

According to Jesus, in verse 24, if a person is devoted to money, what is their attitude toward God?

_____

_____

Read Matthew 6:26-33. For those who choose to serve God rather than money, what assurance do we have regarding our physical needs?

_____

_____

_____

A second, less obvious manifestation of this symptom is compulsive saving. Although saving can be wise and is very much in keeping with biblical principles (Proverbs 21:20), this extreme form of saving tends to harm families and relationships by sending the clear message that money is more important than those we love. Many Christians, men in particular, become obsessive about accumulating money for some future purpose, usually retirement, to the extent that there's never any extra money available for family dates or other activities that bond parents and their children together. The early warning sign for this symptom is making the maximum allowable contribution to your employer's retirement savings plan while the family struggles each month just to make ends meet. In this case the Lord has provided more than sufficient income to meet the family's needs but the funds are misappropriated. As a result, the children never experience the joy of a night at the movies or pizza parlor, day trips to historic sites, or a meaningful family vacation.

REFLECT

When you were a child growing up, what was your family's attitude toward spending money on family activities?

_____

_____

In what ways, if any, has that attitude impacted your current view of "investing" in the needs of those you love?

_____

_____

We must remember that the biblical command to provide for our families (1 Timothy 5:8) requires attention not only to their physical needs, but to their emotional and spiritual needs as well. One of my greatest joys in life is dating my wife and children. Whether I spend time with each one separately or we are all together as a family, this time is invaluable in the strengthening of our relationships and our growing together in Christ. Discipling Lori and our children is a precious gift which requires not only my time, but occasionally my financial resources as well. Although saving as early as possible for retirement makes good economic sense, it is surely not worth sacrificing time and memories with our loved ones. Saving is a very important part of biblical stewardship, but it doesn't supersede the other principles, such as giving, repaying our debts, and providing for the needs of our families. When family suffers because we insist on saving more than we can really afford, we need to check our motivation and priorities. As for me, I would much rather work an extra few years beyond my anticipated retirement age than forego this wonderful time with my wife and children.

REFLECT

Describe an experience in your life in which you, or someone you know, was negatively impacted by compulsive saving.

_____

_____

_____

_____

A third manifestation of the love of money is what the Bible refers to as "covetousness." This habit is relatively easy to recognize in that those suffering from it engage in unending dialogue concerning other people's possessions, such discussions usually characterized by at least a hint of envy. This is the sin that leads to the harmful practice of "keeping up with the Joneses," and the result is often an inordinate amount of consumer debt. If a few neighbors have recently purchased new cars, we suddenly feel the need to buy a car. If a friend moves to a nicer neighborhood, our home begins to appear too old or too small. In short, we want what everyone else has.

Prior to becoming a Christian I had perfected the art of covetousness. The result in my marriage was extreme insecurity for Lori as she constantly wondered where we would find the money to pay for everything I felt I had to have. There was never any significant savings and we often couldn't afford even the most basic necessities because our lifestyle usually exceeded our means. I have also seen the opposite situation, in which a wife has coveted material possessions and constantly pushed her husband for newer and nicer things. The result in this case is a feeling of woeful inadequacy for the husband, who lives with the fear that he will never be able to make his wife happy. This is a devastating situation for a husband and can destroy his confidence in his ability to provide for his family.

DISCOVER

Some of the common things that we might tend to covet are identified in the following passages.

Deuteronomy 5:21 (list three):

1. _____ 2. _____ 3. _____

Joshua 7:21 (name the modern equivalents):

1. _____ 2. _____

According to Romans 7:8, what is the source of our covetous desires?

_____

_____

_____

Overcoming the love of money is an immense challenge and can only be accomplished by God's grace and a firm commitment to His principles. This first symptom of materialism can be the most damaging because it usually impacts our family relationships. As the apostle Paul said to Timothy, in those immortal words spoken twenty centuries ago: *The love of money is a root of all kinds of evil. Some people, eager for money, have wandered from the faith and pierced themselves with many griefs* (1 Timothy 6:10).

Symptom 2: Lack of Generosity

Unlike the first symptom, which directly affects those around us, the second symptom of materialism tends to have a more internal impact. The result is that we often lack joy, and we miss out on the many blessings that derive from a spirit of generosity. A good example of this symptom is described in James 2:15-16: *Suppose a brother or sister is without clothes and daily food. If one of you says to him, "Go, I wish you well; keep warm and well fed," but does nothing about his physical needs, what good is it?* Materialism doesn't cause us not to care about those in need; it simply keeps us from being willing to help. It is a matter of our priorities.

REFLECT

What is your usual initial response when you encounter a person with physical needs who is seeking help (i.e., food, clothing, money)?

_____

_____

This is another area with which I struggled as a new Christian. Since I had created a lifestyle that easily consumed all that I earned, using part of my income to occasionally help those in need was a foreign concept. As I grew in my faith and became more aware of the many needs of families both inside and outside the church, I felt a growing compassion for those who were hurting. However, that compassion rarely, if ever, translated into my actually providing material assistance. As in James's example, I was quick to wish someone well, even pray for them, during their time of trial. But help purchase groceries? Or shoes for their children? It simply wasn't a consideration. Meeting my own needs was my number-one priority. When money was already tight every month, how could I possibly be expected to help others?

Even as I studied God's Word and developed a conviction about providing such assistance, I reasoned that such generosity was to be the work of the wealthy. I fell into the common trap of sinful, human reasoning: *If God wants me to help others He can certainly increase my income.* Have you ever tried that one? Here I was, mindlessly spending all I earned (and more) on my insatiable material appetite, only to blame God for my supposed inability to help those less fortunate. It was only when our family went through great financial difficulty that I learned the difference between "needs" and "wants." I recognized then how much money I had been wasting and how many precious opportunities I had missed to be a blessing to others, not because I lacked sufficient income but because I lacked a generous spirit.

DISCOVER

Read Proverbs 11:25 and 22:9. What benefits does God promise to those who demonstrate a generous spirit?

A generous man will _____ **(Proverbs 11:25).**

A generous man will be _____ **(Proverbs 22:9).**

The lack of generosity is a symptom of materialism because it indicates a self-centered attitude toward income and expenditures. Whereas the love of money leads to a constant striving for more, the lack of generosity causes us to relentlessly guard what we already have. Our priority system looks like this:

> 1. My current needs
> 2. My current wants
> 3. My future needs
> 4. My future wants
> 5. Anything I missed
> 6. The needs of others

As you might imagine, very few dollars will find their way to the last category.

COMMIT

Think of someone you know who is struggling financially. Make a commitment to find out at least one specific need they have (i.e., help with the utility bill, clothing for a child, an auto repair, etc.) and to help meet that particular need. Depending on the cost, you might need to enlist the help of several friends. If you do this, you will be blessed!

Symptom 3: Lack of Contentment

Do you remember the attitude of the Israelites on their journey from bondage in Egypt to the Promised Land? During more than four hundred years of bitter slavery under the whips of their Egyptian taskmasters, the children of Israel cried out to God for deliverance from their oppressors. *God heard their groaning and he remembered his covenant with Abraham, with Isaac and with Jacob* (Exodus 2:24), and He sent the deliverer, Moses, to lead them out of Egypt. To begin to understand the overwhelming joy that God's people experienced upon their deliverance, take a look at the song they sang to their heavenly Father in Exodus 15. It took only three days in the desert, however, for their joy to end and the grumbling to begin (Exodus 15:24).

DISCOVER

Read Numbers 21:4-8. In addition to Moses, who else were the Israelites grumbling against?

_____

_____

_____

How did God respond to this lack of contentment?

_____

_____

_____

_____

_____

Why do you think He responded so severely?

_____

_____

_____

_____

_____

I'm not suggesting that it would be fun to wander in the desert for forty years on a steady diet of manna, manna, and more manna. But anything should be better than four hundred plus years of hard labor and oppression. Rather than daily praising their Father in heaven for His glorious provision of their daily needs, the children of Israel developed the rather unpleasant habit of complaining about the things they didn't have. It's not much of an exaggeration to suggest that God's people grumbled all the way from Egypt to the Promised Land. Lack of contentment was definitely an issue. Sound familiar?

Although similar in many ways, this symptom of materialism is different from the sin of covetousness. Rather than desiring, or coveting, what other people have, those lacking contentment are simply never satisfied with what God has already provided. The result is an absence of joy and gratitude, accompanied by a very shallow walk with our Lord. Although we believe Jesus' promise that if we seek first His kingdom and His righteousness, all our physical needs will be provided for (Matthew 6:33), we tend to view His provision as covering only the barest of necessities. No matter what God gives us, it's never quite what we wanted. Like the Israelites in the desert all those years ago, we grumble and complain. Rather than see God's loving hand in the many things that we daily take for granted, we see only the things we lack. Many of our sentences begin with, "Yeah, but...." Have you ever tried to rejoice with a friend whom God has just supplied with a much-needed car and gotten the response, "Yeah, but it's only a four-cylinder." Or a long-prayed-for larger home? "Yeah, but it's only three bedrooms." New oven? "Yeah, but it seems to overcook everything." Such responses are evidence of a lack of contentment.

REFLECT

List one example of something God has provided for you but with which you have become dissatisfied.

_____

_____

How might this current lack of contentment lead to a future financial problem?

_____

_____

_____

Folks who struggle with discipline in their spending often suffer from a lack of contentment. There's a sense of emptiness that seems to dissipate, at least temporarily, whenever something new is bought. Shortly thereafter, however, the thrill of the new purchase is gone and the emptiness returns with greater intensity. Although I had experienced the extreme version of this malady prior to coming to faith in Christ, I have met numerous Christians over the years who continue to fight this battle. In addition to experiencing a rather lifeless relationship with the Lord, there is an accompanying tendency to accumulate a dangerous amount of credit-card debt as endless material things are purchased to fill a need that only Jesus can truly satisfy.

If you find yourself in a constant battle with one or more of the symptoms of materialism described in this chapter, don't despair. I'm convinced that the solution for all of us lies in a proper understanding of what God's Word has to say about money and possessions. That is the purpose of this book: to help you develop a biblical perspective about your finances and to provide very practical instruction for implementing these principles as you learn them. I promise that if you follow the very basic steps outlined in this book, you will experience a sense of financial freedom that you may not have thought possible. As you continue in this study, please spend time in prayer asking the Lord to open your heart to His truth, and to help you apply this information to your specific circumstances.

STUDY QUESTIONS

1. Refer back to the way you allocated the hypothetical $15,000 at the beginning of the chapter. Does your list indicate a balance between giving, saving, spending, and debt repayment? Or do your priorities suggest a tendency toward materialism?

_____

_____

_____

_____

2. How might the way your parents handled money be influencing your current financial practices?

_____

_____

_____

_____

3. What are the three symptoms of a materialistic lifestyle?

_____

_____

_____

_____

4. How might you be able to tell that your prudent savings plan has evolved into "compulsive" saving? What impact could this have on your friends and family?

_____

_____

_____

_____

5. What is the difference between the sin of covetousness and a sinful lack of contentment?

_____

_____

_____

_____

6. When we find ourselves complaining about, and dissatisfied with, the things we have, who is it that we are ultimately "grumbling" against?

_____

_____

_____

_____

-2-
OWNERSHIP

*"What shall I do? I have no place to store **my** crops.... This is what I'll do. I will tear down **my** barns and build bigger ones, and there I will store all **my** grain and **my** goods."*

           —The Rich Fool, Luke 12:17-18, emphasis mine

*"**Yours**, O Lord, is the greatness and the power...for everything in heaven and earth is **yours**.... Wealth and honor come from **you**.... All of it belongs to **you**."*

           —King David, 1 Chronicles 29:11-12,16, emphasis mine

As I began to study what God's Word had to say about money and possessions, I was immediately struck by the dramatic contrast between the world's view and the biblical view. As one who earlier in life was obsessed with the accumulation of material wealth, I already had a clear understanding of the world's system. It was the emptiness and despair that resulted from "success" in this system that led me to the Cross of Jesus Christ. Like the rich man in Jesus' parable, I wanted everything to be *mine*. Money, after all, was the means of attaining true happiness – or so I had come to believe. My wife, Lori, recently found a wonderful magazine piece that perfectly describes my former attitude toward money and material possessions:

> *THE TODDLER'S CREED*
> If I want it, it's mine.
> If I give it to you and change my mind later, it's
>   mine.
> If I can take it away from you, it's mine.
> If I had it a little while ago, it's mine.
> If it's mine it will never belong to anyone else.
> If we're building something together, all the
>   pieces are mine.
> If it even looks like mine...IT'S MINE![1]

Sound familiar? Let's be honest. Does the attitude depicted in *The Toddler's Creed* describe only the toddlers in our society? Or do we all have a little bit of toddler in us, restlessly clinging to material possessions as if our very lives depended on them?

DISCOVER

Read James 4:1-3. What do we do when we cannot have what we want?

_____

_____

Give an example of a "wrong motive" in asking God for something.

_____

_____

_____

_____

I used to think this self-centered worldview was simply the result of our being bombarded with advertisements about things, money, and success. In time, however, I realized that this attitude is actually deeply rooted in our sinful nature. When my daughter, Rachel, was fifteen months old, she added two new terms to her not-so-extensive vocabulary: *mine* and *go away*. These two terms seemed closely linked in her mind because whenever someone wandered within a few feet of something that she thought belonged to her, the first warning was a screeching "MINE!" Should the violating party fail to realize their error and continue in their path, she would follow up with a more insistent "GO AWAY!" How was it that this precious child, not old enough to have even been mildly exposed to the world's way of thinking, could guard her toys with a ferocity more befitting a mother lion protecting her cubs? It is the human condition.

Perhaps years of repetitive advertising and clever marketing schemes have exacerbated the problem in our society today, but I dare say we have been rather easy prey. As the apostle Paul so astutely noted, in our sin we have willingly *exchanged the truth of God for a lie, and worshiped and served created things rather than the Creator* (Romans 1:25). This was the life I had chosen prior to embracing our Savior. I was trying desperately to fill the emptiness in my heart with money and material things.

It was a frightening experience, indeed, when I finally had everything that I wanted and was no more content with my life than when I had nothing. In fact, it was actually worse because now I had the pressure of the monthly payments on all my stuff! The goal was financial freedom but, strangely, it was becoming evident that financial freedom has very little to do with how much money one has or doesn't have.

REFLECT

Share an example of a purchase you made because you were feeling sad, depressed, or empty.

_____

_____

How did you feel after the purchase was made?

_____

_____

If a person were to struggle regularly with this pattern, what might the long-term result be?

_____

_____

_____

Let's examine this contrast (the world's view vs. the biblical view) in several areas of our financial life. Consider the issue of our *priorities*. The world's view encourages us to pursue the acquisition of personal wealth, putting our trust in worldly treasure. The Bible, on the other hand, tells us to store up our treasures in heaven (Matthew 6:19-21). What about our *purpose*? In the world's system we use money to exalt ourselves, while the Bible teaches that money should be used to glorify God (1 Chronicles 29:10-13). Then there is the issue of *possessions*. The world exhorts us to accumulate; the Bible encourages us to give (Deuteronomy 15:11). How about *debt*? The world would have us believe that debt provides freedom, but the Bible makes it clear that debt creates bondage (Proverbs 22:7). Finally, and the area to which I'll devote most of this chapter, is the difference regarding our *position*. The world's view holds that we are owners, whereas God has assigned us the position of stewards. Let's consider this issue in greater detail.

God's Position

If I were asked to sum up, in three words or less, the most important biblical principle concerning money and possessions it would be this: God owns everything. As simple as this may sound, its truth can be life-changing. Although my initial study was intended to focus solely on a biblical view of money, I found this idea of God's ownership so intriguing that I decided to investigate it separately. What exactly is the "everything" of which God has claimed ownership? The answer was as interesting as it was extensive.

DISCOVER

Write out the following passages next to each aspect of our lives of which God has claimed ownership:

Money — Haggai 2:8

_____

_____

Possessions — Psalm 50:10,12b

_____

_____

Ability — Deuteronomy 8:18

_____

_____

Self — Romans 14:8

_____

_____

This is just a sampling of the verses pertaining to God's ownership, but I think you get the idea. We may not like it, but the Lord could not have spoken more clearly. Every aspect of our lives, everything that we are, have, and do, belongs to God. Keep in mind that this is not simply the opinion of some pastor, professor, or financial counselor — this is truth revealed by the very Creator of life Himself. God owns everything!

If you find this truth difficult to accept, imagine the reaction of a lifelong materialist (me) who had devoted a significant portion of his life trying to increase his inventory of "toys." It was difficult to comprehend at first, but all these things with which I had surrounded myself were really not mine at all. On the authority of God's Word I had to acknowledge that all of it belonged to Him. What's more, God claims ownership not only of all these material things, but clearly states that I belong to Him as well.

A New Perspective

I couldn't be sure exactly what this meant for my life, but it was at the same time both convicting and liberating. One thing that I immediately realized is that I had never "consulted" with God concerning any of these purchases since all were acquired prior to my coming to faith in Christ. Although I couldn't change the past, I was compelled to wonder what my Lord might have said had I known Him at the time and asked His opinion of the lifestyle I was pursuing. This was a radically new way of thinking, but I was certainly intrigued. Would I have bought that too large, too expensive home if I had to first discuss the purchase with my heavenly Father? That would have been an interesting discussion.

> *"Lord, I really need to buy this new home. I know it seems kind of big for us, but we'll probably have a lot more kids, and I really want to be able to entertain guests. Well, I know I don't really enjoy entertaining guests, but I'll probably*

change eventually, and we need to be prepared. What? Down payment? Well, since I don't have any money, I thought I would just take out a home equity loan on this house (You know, the one we've been unable to sell) and use that money to buy the new one. I know the Bible doesn't promote the use of debt, but interest rates were probably much higher when that Book was written. What will I do with Your other house, the one that we're living in now? Oh, You'll love my idea for that. I figured that, since we couldn't sell it, You must want me to own a rental property. We decided to rent it to our friends! What? Oh, the negative cash flow. I did some calculating, and it won't be much more than $500 a month. I know that sounds like a lot but I can sure use a good tax write-off. The mortgage payment on the new home? Well, I know it doesn't look good on paper, but I really think my business is about to pick up. A little more income and we'll be fine, You'll see. I'm sure it won't be a problem. Well, Lord, what do You think?"
What would you have thought?

REFLECT

These were the actual circumstances surrounding the purchase of my dream home. Write some of the obvious reasons that this purchase was foolish:

1. _____
2. _____
3. _____
4. _____
5. _____

This is why I said that my understanding the biblical truth of God's ownership was both convicting and liberating. On the one hand, it was very convicting to think back through every major purchase and deal with both my faulty motives and poor decision-making. At the same time I was uplifted to realize that God's counsel would almost certainly have kept me safe from the difficult financial circumstances in which I suddenly found myself. By the time of my conversion I had accumulated the following: my dream home on a three-and-three-quarter-acre wooded lot, a "rental" home, a condo at the beach, a built-in swimming pool, and two brand new cars. Sound impressive? In addition I had also acquired four mortgages totaling just under $500,000, car loans in excess of $50,000, and consumer debt close to $20,000.

What a life! While friends and colleagues would pat me on the back and tell me how successful I was, I went to work each day in anguish, wondering if my monthly commissions would be sufficient to cover my extravagance. My six-figure income seemed like a lot until I realized that I also had a six-figure lifestyle. I started to realize that many people I knew who earned significantly less were in much better shape financially than I was. And they certainly had less stress in their lives.

DISCOVER

Read Proverbs 28:22. What kind of man is eager to get rich? _____
What is the result of his effort? _____

Never forget this important principle: ***It doesn't matter how much you earn...what matters is how much you spend.*** I've known people who earned several hundred thousand dollars a year and owned absolutely nothing. We've all seen examples of professional athletes who earn multimillion dollar contracts, only to eventually retire with nothing to show for their on-field success. Although the dollars involved were much smaller, this was my experience also. Every few years I lived in a nicer, larger home and drove newer automobiles, but I never actually had a net worth. It stands to reason that if every dollar earned is spent on maintaining a lifestyle, there is nothing left for debt reduction, savings, or investment. It could be argued that simply making the monthly loan payments (mortgage, cars) will increase a family's net worth because as debt declines, equity increases. However, most families that are accustomed to pursuing a lifestyle that is at or above their means will never live in the same home long enough to significantly reduce the mortgage balance. As was true in my case, pursuing the things of this world usually results in frequent exchanges of homes and automobiles. Any equity recognized from paying down the mortgage loan is quickly erased by the payment of selling commissions on the "old" home and closing costs on the new.

New cars are even more costly because they tend to lose value much more quickly than the loan can be repaid. Folks with materialistic tendencies focus on affording the monthly payment, not the price of the car. As a result, three years later when there's a craving for another new car, the amount owed is greater than the trade-in value. The result? No problem, just add the deficit on to the new loan. Just as long as I can handle the monthly payment. Sound familiar? Please forgive my adding salt to the wound!

REFLECT

Consider the statement, "It doesn't matter how much you earn…what matters is how much you spend." Do you agree or disagree? Why?

_____

_____

_____

_____

_____

How have you seen it proved (or disproved) in your own life?

_____

_____

_____

_____

_____

A Proper Response

Being thoroughly convinced that God owns everything, I was left with two burning questions. The first will be dealt with in the next chapter: If God's position is that of "Owner," what then is our position? The second question was perhaps even more perplexing to this recovering materialist: How would God have me _respond_ to this knowledge? I wondered whether the fact of God's ownership would impact my daily life, or if I would just shrug my shoulders and go on handling money the way I always had.

As I considered God's ownership of all things I couldn't help but compare this issue with my conversion to Christ. Many people hear the Gospel, but not all respond to

God's free gift of salvation. Once we've confessed with our mouth that Jesus is Lord, and believe in our hearts that God raised Him from the dead, we are saved (Romans 10:9) and forever cleansed of our sin. What is the proper response to God's amazing grace? Gratitude! Joyful, heartfelt gratitude. Thanksgiving and praise to our loving Savior, who purchased for us that which we could never have purchased for ourselves. Indeed, we respond to God's abundant grace in redeeming us with sincere thankfulness, and it is in this attitude of thanksgiving that our daily lives are forever changed.

In the same way, the proper response to the biblical principle of God's ownership is joyful thanksgiving. I can honestly say that I never truly appreciated having a car until I realized that it belonged to God and that He had provided it to meet my family's transportation needs. The same is true of the home in which my family lives. Whether I rent or buy, the home belongs to God, and He has graciously allowed us use of it. I began to understand that this is the reason most Christians cannot enjoy a meal without first giving thanks to God. This isn't merely a man-made habit or tradition devoid of any meaning. On the contrary, it is the heartfelt response of God's children who recognize that it is He who is providing the food that is needed to sustain them. Look around you for a moment and consider how the Lord has provided for your needs. Everything you see belongs to your heavenly Father, and has been lovingly provided to meet your needs (and even some of your wants!).

REJOICE

Spend a few moments in prayer, giving thanks to the Lord for His provision for your daily needs. Identify several specific things that God has graciously provided for you and give Him glory and praise.

This can be life-transforming. Prior to my conversion I often lamented the many things that I didn't have. No matter how much I accumulated it was never enough. Now, suddenly, I was beginning to appreciate even the smallest things, those which I had taken for granted for years. Do you ever find yourself complaining about something that you want but don't have? Or worrying about things that you need but can't afford? Trust that your loving Father will provide everything you need when you need it. *"See how the lilies of the field grow,"* Jesus said. *"They do not labor or spin. Yet I tell you that not even Solomon in all his splendor was dressed like one of these. If that is how God clothes the grass of the field, which is here today and tomorrow is thrown into the fire, will he not much more clothe you, O you of little faith?"* (Matthew 6:28-30). Indeed, my Father has never failed to provide food for me to eat or clothes for me to wear. He has given me a car to drive, money for gas and insurance, a job through which this money can be earned, and the ability to do the job He provided. It is all His, and He has allowed me the use of it for a time. Our God is faithful!

I resolved, therefore, to live a life of joyful thanksgiving, daily recognizing the grace of God in providing for all of my family's needs. Instead of dwelling on the things that I don't have, I praise God for His faithful provision of all that I do have. Having spent most of my adult life chasing after money and material wealth, I have finally found financial peace and contentment. As a former "lover of money" I can testify to the profound truth spoken by Solomon in the book of Ecclesiastes: *Whoever loves money never has money enough; whoever loves wealth is never satisfied with his income. This too is meaningless* (5:10). Amen!

STUDY QUESTIONS

1. What is your personal response to the idea of God's ownership of everything?

_____

_____

_____

2. How will acknowledging God's ownership of everything affect your future decisions with regard to major purchases?

_____

_____

_____

3. With regard to "storing up our treasures," what is the difference between the biblical view and the world's view?

_____

_____

_____

4. What are some of the specific things in our lives of which God claims ownership?

_____

_____

_____

5. How is it possible for a family with a modest income to accumulate wealth more rapidly than a family with a much higher income?

_____

_____

_____

6. Were there any financial principles presented in this chapter that you are learning for the first time? If so, which?

_____

_____

_____

- 3 -
STEWARDSHIP

Not long after that, the younger son got together all he had, set off for a distant country and there squandered his wealth in wild living. After he had spent everything, there was a severe famine in that whole country, and he began to be in need.

—Parable of the Prodigal Son, Luke 15:13-14

His master replied, "Well done, good and faithful servant! You have been faithful with a few things; I will put you in charge of many things. Come and share your master's happiness!"

—Parable of the Talents, Matthew 25:21

I first entered the financial industry as a stockbroker in 1985. Early in my career I served a client with an unusual and interesting set of circumstances. The size of the account was several million dollars, and this client had a number of similar-sized accounts at other brokerage firms in the same city. What was unusual about the account is that the gentleman I worked with had a power-of-attorney to make all investment decisions, but none of the money actually belonged to him. He was a certified public accountant, had his law degree, and was quite astute with regard to the financial markets. As a result, he had been hired by a wealthy widow, the owner of the estate, to manage all of her financial affairs. One of this gentleman's greatest talents was his ability to negotiate discounted commissions. It was maddening! Typically, he would call and get a price quote on certain bonds that were of interest. Asking the amount of commission that was assumed in the price, he would immediately begin bargaining for a better deal. If he wasn't satisfied that the final offer was as good as it should be, he would simply call one (or several) of his other brokers and give them the opportunity to offer a better price. He would make as many calls as necessary in order to get the lowest possible price. I remember one particularly painful negotiating session where, though I kept my composure, I wanted to cry out, "Why do you care? It's not your money!"

Thinking back, I recognize exactly why he cared. That was precisely what he had been hired to do. He knew none of the money belonged to him, but it didn't matter. Why? Because he was ultimately accountable to the person who did own the money. And his ability to keep his job, or perhaps earn even greater responsibility, was dependent on how well he performed this task and how pleased the owner was with his efforts. We should all be so diligent in handling our financial affairs.

This story came back to me early in my Christian walk as I studied this issue of stewardship. We discussed in the previous chapter that God has clearly stated His rightful position as Owner of all things. Our position, then, as defined by the Word of God, is that of a steward. A simple definition of a *steward* is "one who acts as a supervisor or administrator, as of finances or property, for another."[1] In the example outlined above, the owner was the widow to whom the estate belonged. My client served as the steward of the estate, meaning that he made all financial decisions including expenses, investments, and charitable giving. The steward was accountable to the owner for the management of those resources, and the steward's opportunity for gaining increased responsibilities was directly related to his faithfulness in executing this charge. This is the essence of stewardship.

REFLECT

Describe a situation in your life, past or current, in which you were asked to care for, or manage, something that belonged to another person (to whom you became accountable).

_____

_____

_____

_____

_____

Before examining this important topic as it is described in God's Word, it might be instructive to dispel several myths concerning biblical teaching on finances. There has been a great deal of teaching on this subject in the church but, unfortunately, some of it is very misleading. I don't want to dwell on counterfeit theology, but it is helpful to be warned about errant teaching since it is so often convincingly disguised as truth. Most teaching you will encounter that involves a biblical view of money and possessions will fall into one of three distinct categories: poverty theology, prosperity theology, or stewardship theology. Let's briefly review these three very different teachings and examine the Scripture that is often used in support of each.

Poverty Theology

The thrust of this errant view of Scripture is that, in effect, Christians should be poor. The argument goes that any accumulation of "the things of this world" directly hinders spiritual growth, and the pursuit of such things is a sign of worldliness. Although scriptural support for this position is rather scarce, the most common passage cited is the story of the rich young ruler:

> *A certain ruler asked him, "Good teacher, what must I do to inherit eternal life?" "Why do you call me good?" Jesus answered. "No one is good — except God alone. You know the commandments: 'Do not commit adultery, do not murder, do not steal, do not give false testimony, honor your father and mother.'" "All these I have kept since I was a boy," he said. When Jesus heard this, he said to him, "You still lack one thing. Sell everything you have and give to the poor, and you will have treasure in heaven. Then come, follow me." When he heard this, he became very sad, because he was a man of great wealth. Jesus looked at him and said, "How hard it is for the rich to enter the kingdom of God! Indeed, it is easier for a camel to go through the eye of a needle than for a rich man to enter the kingdom of God."*
>
> —Luke 18:18-25

Leaving the exposition of this passage to those more qualified, I'll simply make a few points that refute the use of Jesus' encounter with this young ruler as support for the poverty theology. There are three aspects of Jesus' teaching that convince me He was not expounding the virtues of universal poverty among the family of faith.

1. SIN OF COVETOUSNESS: The Ten Commandments are often broken down into two categories, those which involve our responsibility to God and those which involve our responsibility to one another.

TO GOD	TO MAN
• You shall have no other gods before Me.	• Honor your father and mother.
• Do not worship or make idols.	• Do not commit murder.
• Do not take the Lord's name in vain.	• Do not commit adultery.
• Remember the Sabbath and keep it holy.	• Do not steal.
	• Do not bear false witness.
	• Do not covet your neighbor's property.

These two categories are summed up in the Great Commandment: " *'Love the Lord your God with all your heart and with all your soul and with all your mind,'* " as Jesus said in Matthew 22:37. *"This is the first and greatest commandment. And the second is like it: 'Love your neighbor as yourself.' All the Law and the Prophets hang on these two commandments"* (verses 38-40). In His discourse with the young ruler, Jesus chose to deal with the second category of commandments, that is, those involving our responsibility to one another.

DISCOVER

Review Luke 18:18-25. Which specific commandments did Jesus instruct the young ruler to obey?

1. _____

2. _____

3. _____

4. _____

5. _____

Now compare this list to the second category of commandments noted above. Which commandment is conspicuous by its absence?

_____

How wonderful is Jesus' ability to go right to the heart of the issue. As you can see, the commandment missing (temporarily) from Jesus' list is the very one this would-be follower of our Lord appears to have been struggling with: covetousness. And how did this young man, clearly familiar with God's Law, respond? Did he correct Jesus, letting Him know that He forgot to include the commandment forbidding covetousness? No, somehow that omission slipped his notice. Rather, his response was a simple: *"All these I have kept since I was a boy"* (verse 21). Jesus followed with a much more direct challenge concerning the same area of sin. *"Sell everything you have and give to the poor, and you will have treasure in heaven. Then come, follow me"* (verse 22).

DISCOVER

Review Matthew 6:24. How does this passage apply to the choice facing the rich young ruler?

_____

_____

There is a clear choice: follow your wealth or follow your Savior. Sadly, this young man who came to Jesus seeking the way to eternal life chose to walk away from the only One who could provide it. *"I am the way and the truth and the life,"* Jesus said in John 14:6. *"No one comes to the Father except through me."* Jesus' message concerning the way to eternal life was unchanging. Far from teaching a poverty theology, the story of the rich young ruler deals with the sin of covetousness and the tremendous difficulty that the rich have in putting their trust in Christ rather than in their riches.

2. ISOLATED INSTRUCTION: Jesus spent a good deal of time addressing how we are to live. If His intended teaching was that His followers should pursue a life of poverty, it is fair to say that such would have been a recurring theme. On the contrary, there are numerous examples throughout the Scriptures, most notably Solomon, of God's pouring out material blessing upon His children.

DISCOVER

Read 2 Chronicles 1:11-12. How does God's promise to Solomon dispel the notion that all of God's people are to live in poverty?

_____

_____

A consistent exhortation throughout the Word of God is for people of faith to give generously to support those who are poor and needy. Just as God graciously provides the ability to work as a means of caring for ourselves and for our families, He expects us to use part of that earned income to help meet the needs of those who are struggling or unable to provide for themselves. This subject of giving will be discussed at length in the next two chapters, but the point I want to make is that God will often provide more than we need so that we can demonstrate His love and mercy by giving to others.

DISCOVER

Read 2 Corinthians 8:13-14. Why does God bless some of His people with excess resources?

_____

_____

Read 2 Corinthians 9:11. What is the end result of this kind of generosity?

_____

Imagine the state of the poor and needy in the church if all believers in our Lord Jesus Christ were to adopt the poverty theology. We would scarcely be able to provide for our own families as commanded in 1 Timothy 5:8, let alone having excess to share with our brothers and sisters in need. It was a wealthy follower of Christ, in fact, who was blessed to provide the tomb in which our Savior was buried. Joseph of Arimathea, a member of the Sanhedrin, was described by Matthew as a _rich man...who had himself become a disciple of Jesus_ (Matthew 27:57). As a member of the Council which was responsible for the brutal death of our Savior, Joseph's reputation might have been forever stained with guilt by association. Instead, his name is memorialized in three Gospels, not only noted for providing the tomb and for being a true believer in our Lord, but also exonerated from blame in Jesus' crucifixion. Luke tells us that Joseph _had not consented to their decision and action_ (Luke 23:51). By God's grace, Joseph was an example of a "rich man" who entered the kingdom of heaven.

REFLECT

Share an example from your own life in which a person with excess resources gave generously to help meet the needs of someone who was struggling financially.

_____

_____

_____

God owns everything, and He will prosper (materially) those whom He chooses to prosper. To suppose that one person is more spiritually mature than another person simply because he has fewer possessions simply doesn't line up with the whole counsel of Scripture, let alone this particular passage.

3. INSTRUCTION TO AN UNBELIEVER: Perhaps the most compelling reason to reject the notion that Jesus was promoting a poverty theology for His children is that this instruction to _"sell everything"_ was not given to one of His followers. The rich young ruler may have gone away _"sad"_ (Matthew 19:22), but he went away nonetheless. As was true with many to whom Jesus preached about the kingdom and eternal life, this young man chose to reject Him. Contrast this encounter with others in which Jesus discussed the path to eternal life. In John's gospel we see several instances in which Jesus directly addresses this issue.

DISCOVER

Read John 3:14-16. In Jesus' discussion with Nicodemus, to what did He point as the way to eternal life?

_____

_____

Similarly, how did Jesus direct the Samaritan woman in John 4:13-14 (also verses 25-26)?

_____

_____

_____

In John 5:24, what instruction did Jesus have for the crowd regarding the path to eternal life?

_____

_____

We should note that in all of these cases Jesus pointed directly to Himself, *not* to the abandonment of possessions, as God's provision for eternal life. We might wonder, then, why Jesus dealt as He did with this young ruler. Why instruct him to abandon all of his possessions? Why not just come out and tell him that he was standing face to face before the long-awaited Messiah? The simple answer is that God's ways are higher than our ways (Isaiah 55:9; Romans 11:33) and many issues will remain a mystery on this side of Christ's return. But perhaps we can glean some insight into Jesus' approach with the young ruler by looking at the parable of the sower found in Matthew 13:1-23, a passage in which Jesus was speaking about the kingdom of God to a large crowd of mostly unbelievers.

In this parable Jesus spoke of a farmer who planted seed in four types of soil. Before offering an explanation of what the parable meant, Matthew tells us, *The disciples came to him and asked, "Why do you speak to the people in parables?"* (verse 10). Jesus went on to explain that His disciples had received *the knowledge of the secrets of the kingdom of heaven* (verse 11), and that *they*, meaning those outside the kingdom (see also Mark 4:11), fulfilled the prophecy of Isaiah in that they would be *ever hearing but never understanding* (Matthew 13:14). Jesus said that, because the hearts of the unbelievers were hardened, He spoke to them in parables so that they could not understand. In the passage regarding the Good Shepherd, Jesus states that *"I know my sheep and my sheep know me"* (John 10:14). Jesus knew when the rich young ruler approached that he was not one of Jesus' sheep, and He spoke to him much as He did to other unbelievers. Whether or not this passage explains Jesus' approach to the young ruler we can only speculate. In any case, it is a highly questionable use of Scripture to assert that Jesus was teaching here a poverty theology which was to be embraced by the family of faith.

In this age of rampant materialism, the poverty theology is not as widespread as it may have been in the past. Certainly, such a teaching would hold little appeal to modern Americans. Today's church in America is much more likely to fall prey to what I consider to be the far more damaging false teaching about money, that which is commonly referred to as the "prosperity gospel."

Prosperity Theology

Although I suspect this movement has always existed to some extent, it seems to have gained prominence during the past two decades. Certainly it is no coincidence that, as the United States has become increasingly prosperous and our culture decidedly self-centered, this materialistic teaching has worked its way into an increasing number of churches. Think about it. Our sinful nature so desires material comfort, wealth, and power. The media feeds these natural tendencies with a persistent message of "you deserve it...you're worth it...you only live once!" Let's face it...the cruise looks great! So do the big-screen TV, the European sports car, the Italian silk suits, and the titanium golf clubs. Our senses are daily bombarded with appeals to our fleshly desires. Eventually we begin to struggle with a longing for things we want but can't afford.

Suddenly, we turn on the TV to see a preacher waving a Bible and insisting that God intends for us to be rich. We're told that God promised to give us whatever we ask for, no strings attached. If we're lacking anything that our materialistic hearts desire, the problem is our lack of faith, not God's unwillingness to give us what we want. The audience is captivated by such boldness. A questionable interpretation of "give and it shall be given to you," and the offering plates are passed among a frenzied crowd who can't seem to get their wallets out fast enough. No wonder the ministries that promote prosperity theology are among the wealthiest ministries in the nation.

DISCOVER

Read 1 Timothy 6:3-10. What does Paul tell us (verse 4) about those who teach that our faith is a means to financial gain?

_____

_____

_____

What has happened to those who have been "eager for money"?

1. _____

2. _____

One passage that is often taken out of context to support prosperity theology is Mark 10:28-31. After the rich young ruler has walked away, Jesus reminds the disciples how difficult it is for the rich to enter the kingdom of heaven. Peter tries to justify himself by reminding Jesus, *"We have left everything to follow you!"* (verse 28). Jesus' response is that *"no one who has left home or brothers or sisters or mother or father or children or fields for me and the gospel will fail to receive a hundred times as much in this present age"* (verses 29-30).

This passage is frequently cited as supporting a concept called the "hundredfold return." Under this teaching, Christians are encouraged to give some amount of money to a particular ministry. They are taught that God promises to bless their gift by returning to them one hundred times the amount given. I've known Christians who have actually borrowed money in order to maximize their gift to such a ministry, believing that God has promised to give them back a hundredfold return on their "investment." How tragic that God's own children, those in whom His Spirit dwells, cannot discern teaching that is so obviously false. *"The spirit indeed is willing, but the flesh is weak"* (Matthew 26:41 KJV).

It is interesting that when Jesus taught that *"no servant can serve two masters"* (Luke 16:13), the two masters He mentioned were God and money. Of all the temptations we would face and all the idols we might worship, Jesus pointed to money as the other master we might seek to serve. In view of the frequently stated fact that there are more verses in the Bible about money and possessions than there are on heaven, hell, prayer, or love, it seems evident that Jesus was warning us that this would be one of our greatest areas of weakness. Perhaps that is why so many of us are vulnerable to prosperity theology. Although we instinctively know this teaching doesn't line up with the whole counsel of God's Word, our flesh desperately wants to believe it.

REFLECT

What impact would you expect this teaching to have on a ministry that promotes prosperity theology?

_____

_____

What impact might it have on the Christians who support such a ministry?

_____

_____

My purpose here is not to make us experts in false theology, but rather to increase our awareness of the heretical teaching that we will almost certainly encounter if we undertake a study of the biblical principles of finance. Our task would have been much less complex had the Lord chosen to put all the information about money in just one book of the Bible. Such verses are scattered throughout God's Word, and much diligence is required in order to derive a well-rounded understanding of this important area. My objective in briefly discussing these two errant positions is, quite simply, to protect us from the false teachers that the apostle Peter cautioned would come among us.

DISCOVER

Read 2 Peter 2:1-3. What term does Peter use to describe those who introduce "destructive heresies" to the church?

_____

What impact will such teaching have on God's people?

_____

_____

What sin motivates these teachers?

_____

How will God ultimately deal with these teachers?

_____

_____

Since the Bible teaches clearly about the dangers of loving money and of worshiping and serving *created things rather than the Creator* (Romans 1:25), why are we so easily and willingly led astray? The apostle Paul had an opinion on that very issue.

DISCOVER

Read 2 Timothy 4:3-4. What kind of teachers does Paul suggest God's people will try to surround themselves with?

_____

_____

What is our motive when we follow false teaching?

_____

When we turn away from the truth, what are we believing?

_____

Those who read this book will likely read others on the same subject. I commend you for seeking an understanding of what the Bible teaches about money, and I pray that the application of the principles shared in this book might impact your life as they have mine. But beware of false teaching. If you begin to read a book, watch a show, or listen to a tape in which this prosperity gospel is being taught, close it, turn it off, or throw it away! If you are aware of such teaching, and sensitive to it, you'll immediately recognize those *who think that godliness is a means to financial gain* (1 Timothy 6:5). Please don't get caught in their trap.

Stewardship Theology

The principle of biblical stewardship is perhaps best described in what is commonly referred to as the parable of the talents, recorded in Matthew 25. Jesus began this parable as follows:

"Again, it will be like a man going on a journey, who called his servants and entrusted his property to them. To one he gave five talents of money, to another two talents, and to another one talent, each according to his ability. Then he went on his journey. The man who had received the five talents went at once and put his money to work and gained five more. So also, the one with the two talents gained two more. But the man who had received the one talent went off, dug a hole in the ground and hid his master's money. After a long time the master of those servants returned and settled accounts with each of them."

—Matthew 25:14-19

This parable goes on to recount the master's response to each servant upon his return. Let's look at how well each servant handled his responsibility and how the master dealt with each of them.

DISCOVER

Read Matthew 25:20-23. What was the master's initial response to the first two servants? Write it out as a quote.

"_____

_____"

_____

What reward was promised as a result of their faithfulness?

_____

_____

Read Matthew 25:24-25. What did the third servant do with his master's money?

_____

What was his motivation for doing so?

_____

_____

Read Matthew 25:26-30. What was the master's initial response to the third servant? Write it out as a quote.

"_____

_____"

In contrast to the rewards given to the first two servants, what were the consequences of the third servant's unfaithfulness?

1. _____
2. _____

What is immediately evident in this parable is the issue of ownership. The master is clearly the owner, and the servants, to whom the master's property was entrusted, are the stewards. So it is with our handling of financial resources. You may remember from the previous chapter that God has claimed ownership of all things. This parable reinforces that concept of God's ownership, as well as the fact that God determines, in His infinite wisdom and purpose, how much will be entrusted to each of us, His servants. There are three important points that must be understood if we are to meet our biblical obligation as stewards of God's resources.

1. THE OWNER HAS RIGHTS; THE STEWARD HAS RESPONSIBILITY.

Understanding this important principle is the first step to becoming a good steward. Since everything that we have comes from God and belongs to God, He alone has the right to do as He pleases with these resources. His rights include, among other things, decisions as to when to entrust His resources to us, how much to entrust to us, and for what period of time they will be entrusted to us. As stewards, we have only the responsibility to properly care for that which our Master has chosen to allow us to use.

We tend to abuse our position as stewards when we begin to treat God's property as if it is our own. For example, discussed at length in the next chapter is the biblical command to share with those who are in need. If I understand that my Master has given me a monthly income which is, in part, intended to help others, the act of giving generously is as natural as paying my own bills. However, if I view all income as if it belongs to me, I am much more likely to spend everything on my own temporal pleasures and ignore those less fortunate. The moment we attempt to usurp God's position as Owner, we immediately risk our loving Father's chastisement as He takes away from us that which has been entrusted to our care. (See Matthew 25:28-29.)

REFLECT

Why is it sometimes difficult for Christians to embrace the truth that God has all the rights and we have only responsibilities?

_____

_____

2. THE STEWARD IS ACCOUNTABLE TO THE OWNER. Accountability can be either a blessing or a curse, depending upon how faithfully we've executed our charge. It is fair to suggest that the first two servants welcomed the opportunity to give an account, and their faithful stewardship was both commended and rewarded. The third steward didn't fare as well, receiving a harsh rebuke and having even the little that had been entrusted to him taken away. We must live with the constant awareness that we will, in fact, give an account to our Master for our use of the financial resources He has entrusted to us.

Equally clear is the fact that this accountability is not affected by the amount He has given us to manage. The steward who was given one talent was held just as accountable as the steward who was given five. It is often our tendency to blame our poor stewardship on a lack of resources, as if God were somehow to blame for our misuse of His money. How often we are tempted to bemoan how little we think we have, or to boast that we would be more than willing to give generously to the Lord's work if only He would give us more to give. But God is not mocked; neither does He make mistakes. He knows precisely the condition of our hearts and how much of His property should be entrusted to each of us. It is interesting that the steward who failed to properly manage the resources entrusted to him was also the steward who was given the least amount to manage in the first place. Coincidence? I think not.

Share an experience from your life in which you were faithful in managing something that had been entrusted to you and were commended by the owner.

_____

_____

Now share a time in which you failed to be a faithful steward and were called to account.

_____

_____

_____

3. "EACH ACCORDING TO HIS ABILITY." I've studied this parable many times and this is still the statement that is most striking to me (Matthew 25:15). It makes perfect sense to me that the steward who is faithful will be entrusted with greater resources and responsibility, and that the unfaithful steward will have these things taken away (verse 29). But this passage teaches that even the amount initially entrusted to each servant was in some way based upon his ability to manage it properly (verse 15). I couldn't help wondering what ability was required and how this ability was demonstrated. This parable gives no such detail; it simply states that each servant was given a specific amount in keeping with his own ability. Since the Bible has so much to say about the proper use and handling of God's resources, we might infer that our adhering to these principles is an indication of our ability in this area.

DISCOVER

Read Psalm 119:33-36. What is one way in which we can increase our ability to exercise faithful stewardship?

_____

It is not uncommon for Christians to eschew learning biblical principles of finance because they feel like they don't have enough money to properly implement them. If my monthly expenditures already meet or exceed my after-tax income, how can I be expected to give generously to the Lord's work, accelerate debt repayment, or build an emergency savings fund so I can stop using credit cards when something breaks? We pray that God will increase our income so we can be better stewards. The Bible teaches that if we aren't good stewards, God probably won't increase our income.

If we aren't already making the best and wisest use of those resources currently entrusted to our care, there is no reason to believe we will somehow do a better job with more. And this passage makes clear that if we are currently lacking in our ability to practice good stewardship, not only will the least amount of additional resources be entrusted to us, but we also run the very real risk of having our existing resources taken away.

COMMIT

Spend the next few moments in prayer asking God to increase your ability to manage His resources. Ask Him to use this study to strengthen your knowledge and understanding of biblical finances, and then make a firm commitment to implement these principles in the management of the resources He entrusts to you.

I would like to close this chapter on stewardship with a practical example. Several years ago, my oldest daughter acquired her driver's license. Since Megan didn't have a car of her own, she had to ask for permission to borrow the family car when transportation was needed. Picture this: I allow Megan to use my car with the agreement that she bring it home by a certain time. It is perfectly clean, inside and out, and the gas tank is full. Off she goes. The set time for her return comes and goes...she's late, very late. Finally, seven hours after curfew, she finally returns home. The car is covered with mud, there are several noticeable new scratches on the hood and a large dent in the rear, just above the now missing taillight. The interior is scattered with food wrappers and cold French fries. The gas tank is empty. Question: How long do you suppose it will be before the car is entrusted to my daughter again?

Thankfully, God blessed us with an extremely responsible daughter in Megan, and we've been spared the common anxieties that often accompany that first driver's license. But the example is instructive for all of us. What would our response likely be if one of our children were to so blatantly abuse the property we entrusted to them? Would we reward such behavior with additional responsibility?

REFLECT

Share an example in which you loaned something to a child or friend and they failed to properly care for it. How did you respond?

_____

_____

Now let's consider the alternative outcome. Let's assume Megan brings the car back earlier than was necessary. The car is washed and waxed, has a full tank of gas, and she even sprayed that stuff that makes the interior smell brand new. Do you think Megan will be allowed to use the car again? You bet! So it is with our management of God's resources.

When God entrusts each of us with His money and possessions, He expects a certain degree of responsibility and accountability. Considering the vast amount of wisdom in the Scriptures on this topic, God has certainly provided the information needed to exercise good stewardship. Our part is to avail ourselves of the information He has provided. As in all other areas of life, the Bible is our owner's manual.

REFLECT

Have you ever tried to assemble something without bothering to read the instructions first? Share an example and the outcome.

_____

_____

As you continue in this study of God's stewardship instructions, please keep in mind the three important principles highlighted in this chapter.

1. God owns everything, and as Owner, He has all of the rights. We, on the other hand, are simply stewards of His resources, and we are given the responsibility of proper management of all that He entrusts to us, be it much or little.

2. As stewards, we are accountable to the Owner for how we handle His resources. With this accountability comes either the Master's blessing for our faithfulness or His condemnation for our unfaithfulness.

3. The amount entrusted to us, both now and in the future, is in some way tied to our ability to manage these resources in accordance with God's stated principles. The most basic means of increasing our ability is to study biblical principles in finance.

Prepare for an exciting journey into the practice of biblical stewardship. My purpose in writing this study is not only to teach us *what* to do with God's money, but more importantly, *how to do it.* If you have never undertaken a study of these principles, or if you've been unsuccessful thus far in their implementation, this study should help you bridge the gap between knowledge and practice. There is great joy, freedom, and contentment ahead as we embrace and apply God's wisdom in this important area of our lives.

STUDY QUESTIONS

1. What is the basic premise of the false teaching known as poverty theology?

_____

_____

2. What problems can arise in the church when such teaching is embraced and practiced?

_____

_____

3. What is the basic premise of prosperity theology?

_____

_____

4. What potential dangers can arise in a church that follows this false teaching?

_____

_____

_____

5. With regard to money and possessions, what is the difference between God's position and our position?

_____

_____

_____

6. What two things directly impact how much God might entrust to us?

_____

_____

_____

7. How might understanding our accountability to God in managing His resources improve the quality of our financial decision-making?

_____

_____

_____

Five Steps
to Financial
Freedom

- 4 -
GIVING
PART 1

"Will a man rob God? Yet you rob me. But you ask, 'How do we rob you?'
In tithes and offerings. You are under a curse — the whole nation of you
— because you are robbing me."

—Malachi 3:8-9

"Bring the whole tithe into the storehouse, that there may be food in my
house. Test me in this," says the LORD Almighty, "and see if I will not throw
open the floodgates of heaven and pour out so much blessing that you will
not have room enough for it."

—Malachi 3:10

This is the starting point in our quest for financial freedom, and these next two chapters will deal with both the biblical teaching on giving and the practical application of these principles. First, we will review the three different levels of giving to which God calls us, and then we will answer some of the most common questions and concerns that Christians have when seeking to implement their giving program.

Not surprisingly, giving is the area that presented the greatest struggle to me as a new Christian. In fact, when I finally undertook the study of this issue it was for the express purpose of *disproving* the concept of tithing. The word *tithe* simply means "10 percent,"[1] and according to God's Word it is the starting point for all Christian giving. I remember how ridiculous this sounded when I first heard of it. Ten percent? Of my whole income? I hadn't spent much time reading the Bible, but I was pretty sure it didn't say that!

REFLECT

When you were first introduced to the concept of tithing, now or in the past, what was your initial response to the thought of giving away 10 percent of your income?

_____

_____

_____

I remember having a conversation with a pastor just a few months after coming to faith in Jesus Christ. I was contemplating the size of his church and the number of members in the congregation. "It must cost a lot of money to operate this church each year," I suggested. "How much of your time has to be spent on fundraising?" He looked at me somewhat amused — obviously I had been watching too much TV — and answered, "We really don't do any fundraising. This church believes in the biblical practice of tithing." He went on to explain that many of the congregants gave generously, and _voluntarily,_ to support the ongoing work of the church. In fact, a large number of these families gave at least 10 percent of their gross income. "But why would they give so much?" I was incredulous. His answer: "That's the instruction God gives us in His Word. Some families give much more than a tithe, and some give less. The amount each family gives is between them and the Lord. These folks give freely because they want to give, because they want to be obedient to God."

I couldn't get that conversation out of my head. To put this into perspective in view of the materialistic lifestyle I had spent so many years pursuing, a tithe on my income was roughly equivalent to the monthly payments on our two new cars plus the payment on the home equity loan we had taken out for the built-in swimming pool. I quickly concluded that this concept of "tithing" was the dumbest thing I had ever heard! But I couldn't stop thinking about it. What could possibly motivate someone to give so much? How could they afford it? It finally bothered me so much that I decided to spend several weeks of my daily devotional time studying this topic. My purpose was simple: Prove that God does _not_ call on His people to give 10 percent of their income to the work of His church. I was determined to put an end to this nonsense once and for all.

Surveys indicate that only a small percentage of evangelical Christians actually tithe. Why do you think that is true?

_____

_____

_____

_____

Although I was very serious in my initial attempt to disprove the principle of tithing, I was even more serious about truly understanding God's perspective. It was very important to me to know exactly what God had to say on the matter of giving. I firmly believed, then as now, that the Bible is the inspired, inerrant Word of God. Although my desire was that the Bible would teach something other than tithing, I was prepared to accept as truth whatever I learned in this study. In other words, if there was a difference between what I believed and what God actually said, I needed to change what I believed. As you read on, I would challenge you to adopt the same posture. Don't accept tithing, or any other doctrine, simply because someone tells you it is so. Search the Scriptures. Commit to a personal study. But then, once you have an understanding of what God teaches, you must accept that position as truth, regardless of whether it conflicts with your prior understanding or belief. As Jesus prayed, *"Sanctify them by the truth; **your word is truth**"* (John 17:17, emphasis mine).

COMMIT

Spend the next few moments in prayer, asking God to open your eyes to His truth about giving. Make a firm commitment to obedience as He teaches you.

As I began my study, I had already manufactured an argument for disregarding the idea of tithing. "We're no longer living under the Law," my reasoning went, "we're living under grace." I suspected that tithing was probably a part of the Old Testament Law which, much like animal sacrifices, no longer needed to be observed. A brilliant argument – or so I thought. In years of teaching on this subject I've since discovered that this is usually the first line of defense that Christians take against the tithe. But even a surface study of God's Word will correct this mistaken view.

Tithing in the Old Testament

My initial surprise came when I discovered that the practice of tithing actually pre-dated the Mosaic Law by at least four hundred years. The first appearance of the word *tithe* in the Bible occurs in Genesis 14. As Abram was returning victorious from a battle he was met by a man named Melchizedek, whom the Bible reports *was king of Salem...He was priest of God Most High* (14:18).

DISCOVER

Read Genesis 14:20. How did Abram respond to the blessing pronounced on him by Melchizedek?

_____

_____

_____

_____

It was common for the victor in battle to bring back the enemy's possessions, the "spoils" of war. Immediately upon meeting with one of God's representatives, Abram instinctively offered a tithe of all that he was bringing back from the war. The Bible is silent on the origin of this practice, but suffice it to say that it existed long before the Law was given at Mt. Sinai. In fact, although the word *tithe* was not specifically used, it could be argued that the practice goes back at least as far as Cain and Abel.

DISCOVER

Read Genesis 4:2-4. In what way is this passage, and the activity it describes, similar to Genesis 14:20?

_____

_____

Somehow, Cain and Abel both understood that all of their increase came from the Lord, and that a portion of this increase was to be given back to Him. The two brothers seemed to already be engaging in a practice that wasn't defined until much later in God's Word.

A third example of tithing occurs in Genesis 28. God appeared to Jacob in a dream and confirmed the covenant He had made with Abraham (formerly Abram). God promised to bless Jacob and his descendants, and Jacob's instinctive response was not unlike that of his grandfather, Abraham, in the passage noted previously.

DISCOVER

Read Genesis 28:20-22. How did Jacob respond to God's promised blessing?

_____

_____

Consistent with other references to giving throughout the Scriptures, the foundation of this vow was Jacob's understanding that all we have comes from the Lord. Returning to Him the first 10 percent simply acknowledges God's ownership and provision. *"Bring the best of the firstfruits of your soil to the house of the LORD,"* God instructed the Israelites in Exodus 23:19. Throughout history, God's people have understood that they were to honor God by giving back to Him the first and best portion of what He had so graciously provided to them.

Tithing in the New Testament

Although my argument against tithing was quickly losing its validity, I wasn't yet convinced that this practice was still applicable today. Surely if God meant for tithing to be observed by the modern church, there would be evidence in the New Testament as well. Did Jesus have anything to say about tithing? Did any of the New Testament writers address this issue? It didn't take long to answer both questions.

DISCOVER

Read Matthew 23:23. In the midst of His rebuking the Pharisees, what does Jesus say about their practice of tithing?

_____

_____

_____

While Jesus did not elaborate here on the subject of tithing, He clearly affirmed the practice. Even though the Pharisees were ignoring *the more important matters of the law*," Jesus reinforced that they were correct in tithing (Matthew 23:23).

DISCOVER

Read 1 Corinthians 16:1-2. How is the practice described by Paul similar to tithing as it was presented in the Old Testament?

_____

_____

Although the word *tithe* is not specifically used in this passage, it is clearly implied, and this very practice continues to exist in most evangelical churches today. At this point in my study, I had to concede that a clear picture was emerging, albeit a much different picture than I was expecting. God calls on His people to acknowledge His ownership of all things by giving back to Him at least 10 percent of all that He entrusts to us. Tithing is not the only form of giving described in the Scriptures, but it is certainly the starting point. Tithing is a practice that God takes very seriously, a fact that is made very clear in the Old Testament book of Malachi.

DISCOVER

Read Malachi 3:8-9. How does God view Israel's failure to tithe?

_____

_____

What is the result of their disobedience?

_____

If the preceding passages hadn't convinced you, this one certainly should. Tithing is not just a nice idea, a noble gesture reserved for the spiritually mature. God commands tithing, and failure to tithe is tantamount to robbing God. It is interesting that in this same passage, which contains perhaps the Scripture's harshest condemnation against those who fail to tithe, God also promises an incredible blessing to those who obey:

"Bring the whole tithe into the storehouse, that there may be food in my house. Test me in this," says the LORD Almighty, "and see if I will not throw open the floodgates of heaven and pour out so much blessing that you will not have room enough for it."

—Malachi 3:10

What an incredible promise! This passage did not so much motivate my obedience as it did capture my imagination. By the time I had internalized this passage, I was already convinced that God called me to tithe, so this section of scripture, as powerful as it is, did not alter my thinking. What it did accomplish, however, is that it gave me a different understanding of the nature and character of God. My loving Father instructs me to give generously, and then He graciously supplies the money that I'm to give. What's more, when I obediently give as I've been instructed, giving back to God only a small part of what He's given to me, God promises to bless me. Not just a small blessing mind you, but He promises to throw open the floodgates of heaven and pour out so much blessing that there won't be room enough for it (3:10). What a great example of the love and grace of our heavenly Father!

DISCOVER

What specific blessings did God promise Israel in Malachi 3:11-12?

1. _____

2. _____

3. _____

Give examples of what these blessings might look like today (see also Deuteronomy 8:4). What kinds of protection might God provide?

1. _____

2. _____

3. _____

I have always utilized a written budget, and I must confess that tithing did not look good on paper. My overextended lifestyle was already consuming every dollar I was taking in, so finding the money with which to tithe seemed a daunting task indeed. However, I did believe God. If He had called me to tithe, I was determined to do so.

And if He promised to bless my tithe, I was equally determined to take Him at His Word. I couldn't figure out how we were suddenly going to make ends meet on just 90 percent of my income, especially since 100 percent was at times insufficient. But I did believe that God was able to provide, and that He had promised to do so.

REJOICE

Pause for a moment to reflect on God's goodness toward us and His promise of blessing as we obey Him by giving generously to His work. Give Him praise for this glorious truth!

As I continued to study this topic of giving I came quickly to realize that tithing was not the only level of giving prescribed by the Scriptures. There are actually three levels of giving: the tithe, freewill offerings, and sacrificial giving. Having reviewed the biblical support for the tithe, let's look now at what God's Word has to say about the other two levels of giving to which God calls us.

Freewill Offerings

At this point the question might arise: What is the difference between a tithe and a freewill offering? The tithe, as we discussed, is a percentage of our income and is to represent the first and best part of what God has entrusted to us. The freewill offering, on the other hand, usually represents that which is given from our excess resources, and it is an amount given above and beyond the tithe. Freewill offerings can be given to a variety of needs and causes: a special church project (i.e., a building fund), food or clothing for a family in need, ministries outside the local church, or even the sponsoring of a child in a third-world country.

Let's look at several Old Testament accounts of the freewill offering. In Exodus 35 we see Moses beginning to accumulate the resources needed to build the tabernacle.

DISCOVER

Read Exodus 35:4-10. What indication do we have that this giving on the part of God's people was different from the requirement of tithing?

_____

_____

Unlike the tithe, which is a clear command to all Christians, freewill offerings are given voluntarily: _Everyone who is willing is to bring to the LORD an offering of gold, silver and bronze_ (Exodus 35:5). The response of the people is described in similar terms: _Then the whole Israelite community withdrew from Moses' presence, and everyone who was willing and whose heart moved him came and brought an offering to the LORD for the work on the Tent of Meeting_ (Exodus 35:20-21).

REFLECT

Have you ever experienced God's moving your heart with compassion when you saw someone in need? Explain the circumstances and your response.

_____

_____

This would be an example of a freewill offering, a voluntary gift that is given in response to a particular need. As we increasingly experience God's grace and mercy in our own lives, we are often moved to respond with compassion and generosity toward others. In Israel's case, the response to Moses' request for freewill offerings was both inspiring and overwhelming.

DISCOVER

Read Exodus 35:22-27. How did God's people respond to Moses' request? How did the resources they gave compare with what was needed to complete the work?

_____

_____

_____

_____

This is a wonderful picture of freewill offerings. Keep in mind that the people of Israel were already tithing, so their gifts for the construction of the tabernacle were in addition to their regular giving. I suspect that there are very few churches or ministries today that suffer from the challenge of having *too many* resources!

REFLECT

Share an experience you've had with your church or other ministry in which freewill offerings were needed in order to complete the work. How did God's people respond?

_____

_____

_____

Another example of freewill offerings appears in 1 Chronicles 29. In this chapter, David was calling on all of Israel's officers, commanders, and officials to give generously to the work of building the temple. Although God had chosen Solomon, not David, to build the temple, David took upon himself the responsibility of raising the resources that would be needed to do the work. In a demonstration of David's gift for leadership, he first set the example by giving a significant portion of his personal wealth, and then he called on the other leaders to follow his example. Let's look at their response.

DISCOVER

Read 1 Chronicles 29:6,9. What are some of the words used in this passage to describe the attitude with which these offerings were given?

_____

_____

A third example of freewill offerings appears in the second chapter of Acts. In verses 44 and 45 we're told that *all the believers were together and had everything in common. Selling their possessions and goods, they gave to anyone as he had need.* This passage is often misunderstood as teaching a communal lifestyle in which all participants must forsake their personal possessions, which become the property of the group. On the contrary, this passage is a wonderful demonstration of freewill offerings.

This passage is similar to the Great Commission given in Matthew 28:19 which, though most often translated, *Therefore go and make disciples of all nations...*, can also be interpreted, "Therefore, **as you are going**, make disciples of all nations..." (emphasis mine). Using the same principle, Acts 2:45 might be more accurately interpreted to read, "**As they sold** their possessions and goods, they gave to anyone as he had need" (emphasis mine). The issue is not whether the new believers continued to own their own property — property ownership is implicit in the eighth commandment, *Thou shalt not steal.* Rather, as people decided to sell some of their possessions, they made the proceeds available for those among them who were in need. This is the essence of a freewill offering: giving generously, and voluntarily, of the resources that God has entrusted to us.

DISCOVER

Read Acts 2:46-47. What were some of the specific blessings that resulted from God's people living in community and caring for the needs of one another?

_____

_____

_____

_____

Sacrificial Giving

The third level of giving described in the Scriptures is sacrificial giving. Whereas freewill offerings are usually made from our excess funds, sacrificial giving occurs when we give up something we have or need in order to meet the needs of someone else. To describe exactly what sacrificial giving is, it might be helpful to relate an example of what it is not. Once when I took my six-year-old daughter out to breakfast, we found ourselves discussing how many toys and dolls some of her friends have. I asked her what might happen if a child was given everything he or she asked for, and Rebekah astutely answered, "They could become greedy, or not appreciate what they have." I followed up by asking what a child with a lot of toys might do to avoid developing a greedy or ungrateful heart, and she responded, "They could give away some of their toys to children that are poor." Trying to conceal my fatherly pride as I saw my child's seemingly generous heart on display, I asked her which of her own toys she might want to give away to the poor children. She paused thoughtfully, then answered, "The ones I don't play with anymore." Wrong answer!

Rather than squander a teachable moment, I helped her to understand the greater blessing that might result from giving away her *favorite* toys, the ones she played with the most. That would represent one type of sacrificial giving. A more challenging example might be the child who gives away his or her lunch money, choosing to do without, in order to provide a meal for another child who has no money. Or a family who gives up their annual vacation in order to help provide food and clothing for a struggling single mom and her kids.

DISCOVER

Read Luke 21:1-4. How does this passage demonstrate sacrificial giving?

_____

_____

_____

Why did Jesus value the widow's gift above the larger gifts of the wealthy?

_____

_____

_____

Another example of giving that is sacrificial in nature occurs in 2 Corinthians 8, where the apostle Paul describes the generosity of the church in Macedonia. Not only does this passage provide a valuable example of sacrificial giving, but it also instructs us on the heart condition that should accompany this level of giving.

DISCOVER

Read 2 Corinthians 8:2-3. How do we know that the giving by the Macedonian church was sacrificial in nature?

_____

_____

_____

How did Paul characterize their desire to give?

_____

_____

_____

Although giving sacrificially might be considered "giving until it hurts," it is always done with a joyful and thankful heart. One of the greatest blessings that God has given us on this side of eternity is the privilege of sharing in the spread of the Gospel and the making of disciples. The sacrificial giver is motivated, first by having personally experienced the grace and mercy of God in their own life, and then by a desire to make that grace and mercy known to others.

Making the Commitment

I would like to conclude this chapter with a personal illustration. When I first became convicted about my responsibility to tithe, there was absolutely no way I could afford to do so. It just didn't work on paper. We had no excess cash flow and, despite earning a relatively high income at the time, my personal debt and monthly expenses easily consumed every penny I earned. We owned a rental property, a single-family home, which we had previously lived in and were now renting to family members at a significant discount to the average rent in that area. We had a negative cash flow of $500 per month and had been trying to sell the home for over a year. I remember thinking that if God would just sell that home, the money we would save would represent a significant portion of our monthly giving commitment.

Rather than wait for this house to sell, however, my wife and I committed to the Lord that, although we didn't know how, we would begin tithing with the next month's budget. Strangely, within a few days our realtor called with the news that we had a contract on the home. I was so excited I could barely contain myself! The amount offered was very close to the asking price, so we accepted the contract and praised God for His provision. I had understood God's promise to bless the faithful giving of His children, but this was almost too good to be true. I hadn't even written the first tithe check yet, and I already knew where the money would come from. If only this were the whole story.

REFLECT
Have you ever committed to giving without knowing where the funds would come from? Describe the situation.

_____

_____

_____

_____

_____

What seemed like an immediate blessing turned out to be the first test of our commitment to tithing. As I prepared my budget for the coming month, I was delighted to write so large a number in the giving category. Then it happened. On Friday (which was also payday), my realtor called to inform me that the deal had fallen through. The buyer failed to get their financing, which allowed them to back out of our contract. We were back to square one, with no end in sight to the $500 per month negative cash flow on this rental property.

I was devastated. Where was God in this? I had demonstrated my faithfulness by committing to tithing, and now the money I thought God had provided to give away wasn't going to exist. I hate to admit it, but my faith was shaken. The next morning, when it was time to pay the bills, I laid them out neatly on my desk along with the checkbook. My commitment was on the line, and I stared at the checkbook, uncertain as to what I should do. Surely the Lord wouldn't hold me to my commitment now that the sale had fallen through, would He? I convinced myself that God would understand if we put off tithing for awhile. But my conscience wouldn't let go. My heart was convicted about tithing but my head was opposed to doing so until I knew we could afford it. I decided that Lori and I needed to take a long drive in the country. I needed to think this through – and pray.

REFLECT

Share an experience from your life in which you knew what God would have you do but you struggled with obedience.

_____

_____

_____

_____

As we drove along and talked about this situation, I started to understand what the Lord might be teaching me. You see, when I committed to tithing, it wasn't because I had the money, or that I knew where it would come from. My decision was based on my understanding of God's Word. On that basis, how could I now question the decision? Either God calls His people to tithe, or He doesn't. If I was truly persuaded from Scripture that His will is for His people to tithe, then I needed to be obedient. That settled it. God called us to tithe, and my wife and I were going to obey. Our Father promised to bless our giving and to provide for all of our needs, and by faith we were trusting Him to do so. We decided that, as soon as we got home, I would do nothing else until I wrote those tithe checks. Up to that point in my Christian life, this was the most freeing decision I had ever made. I couldn't wait to get home.

We walked in the door and I headed straight to my office, a man on a mission. Just before I sat down at my desk, my daughter handed me my telephone messages. One was from our realtor. You know what was running through my mind, don't you? What if? I now had two things to do: write my tithe checks and call our realtor. Which would come first? I grabbed the phone. I hung it back up. Then I prayed.

Lord, I explained, as if He didn't already know my thoughts, _if I return this call and we find out that, somehow, the deal has been revived and the house is still sold, I'm right back where I started. I'll start tithing, but I'll do so knowing where the money is coming from, and I'll never know how firm my commitment was. But You taught me this morning that my decision to tithe was based on obeying Your Word, not on figuring out in advance how we're going to do it. Please help me to be obedient._

Free at last. With a sense of joy and excitement that I can remember to this day, I opened the checkbook and wrote those checks. I had written many checks in my life, but these were by far the most enjoyable. There was an incredible sense of victory in having obeyed my Lord, and also a sense of wonder. Clearly, God was at work transforming my heart. Several months earlier I was one of the most selfish men I had ever met, the epitome of a lover of money. Now, armed only with a childlike faith and a conviction that God's Word is true, I was giving money away...and enjoying it!

I closed the checkbook and praised God for the privilege of giving to His work. I thanked Him for changing my heart and teaching me the freedom that comes from obedience. Then I picked up the telephone and called our realtor. As you might have guessed, the sale was back on. A relative of the buyer had agreed to help them by providing the funds needed to make settlement, and the bank gave them a commitment for the mortgage. Thirty days later the rental property, along with the $500 per month negative cash flow, was gone and soon to be forgotten. But the lesson I learned about joyful obedience will be with me for the rest of my life.

STUDY QUESTIONS

1. What is the literal meaning of the word *tithe*?

_____

_____

_____

_____

2. Whom does God require to tithe?

_____

_____

_____

_____

3. According to Malachi 3:8, how does God view the failure of His people to tithe?

_____

_____

_____

_____

4. How do freewill offerings differ from the tithe?

_____

_____

_____

_____

5. How would you describe sacrificial giving?

_____

_____

_____

_____

6. What would be an example of giving sacrificially?

_____

_____

_____

_____

7. How has this chapter impacted your view of giving and what (if anything) will you do differently in response?

_____

_____

_____

_____

- 5 -
GIVING
PART 2

"I have seen a grievous evil under the sun: wealth hoarded to the harm of its owner."

—King Solomon, Ecclesiastes 5:13

"One man gives freely, yet gains even more; another withholds unduly, but comes to poverty. A generous man will prosper; he who refreshes others will himself be refreshed."

—King Solomon, Proverbs 11:24-25

In my years of teaching and counseling on the subject of biblical stewardship, I've noticed that five particular questions are consistently asked when the topic of giving is being discussed. This chapter will be devoted to exploring the answers to these five questions regarding giving.

Tithing on Gross vs. Net Income

Should Christians tithe on their gross income or their net income? This is a question that never occurred to me as I studied the Scriptures, so I was surprised at how often it is asked in workshops and seminars. I have been exposed to teaching on both sides of this issue so I believe I understand the logic of those who suggest that it is appropriate and acceptable to tithe on net (after-tax) income. However, I'll preface my remarks by stating with absolute conviction that the Bible is not the least bit ambiguous on this issue: Tithing is to be based on our gross income.

DISCOVER

Read Exodus 23:19, Deuteronomy 26:10, and Proverbs 3:9. What term is used in these passages to describe the portion that we are to give to God?

_____

_____

_____

_____

What do you think this term means?

_____

_____

_____

_____

When I first encountered questions about tithing on the gross or the net income, and particularly when it involved someone's making a defense of tithing on their net income, I quickly noticed that the defense was based exclusively on human logic, as opposed to biblical principles: "How can I be expected to give away 10 percent of money that I never actually receive?" This is, of course, a reference to the fact that most folks receive a paycheck with the taxes already taken out. Sound logical? The money we have to work with each month is our take-home pay. Doesn't it make sense that our tithe should be based on that amount?

My first response is to remind us that taxes, though we are certainly commanded in Scripture to pay them, simply represent a normal monthly outflow. Many of us also must make a mortgage payment each month. In my case, in addition to having my paychecks deposited directly into my checking account, I have my monthly mortgage payment automatically deducted from the same account. I never see the money. Using this line of reasoning, I could also deduct that amount from my take-home pay. How about medical insurance, or my 401K plan contributions? Each is an additional item that reduces the amount of money I have available when I get paid. The fact that most of us have our income taxes automatically deducted from our paychecks doesn't free us from the responsibility to tithe on all of our income. Many workers (such as self-employed, independent contractors) do not have taxes withheld from their paycheck. Instead, they are responsible to make quarterly estimated tax payments. Has God set a different standard of giving for these folks than He has for those whose taxes are automatically withheld, simply because they pay their taxes in a different way? Suffice it to say there is no biblical basis for this position.

REFLECT

Explain how tithing on one's net income would violate the principle of the "firstfruits."

_____

_____

_____

_____

_____

Another argument frequently used to support tithing on one's net income involves the taxes themselves. A significant portion of our tax dollars, the reasoning goes, is given by the government to various welfare programs which are intended to benefit the poor and needy in our land. It would naturally follow that the money withheld from our paychecks for taxes is already being given to help those in need, albeit indirectly. This position, like the first, seems primarily concerned with finding a theological loophole. Giving is seen as a chore, and the objective is to claim obedience to God's command while giving the smallest amount possible.

When we tithe, we are acknowledging God's ownership of all things and His faithful provision of all that we need. We are obediently and joyfully returning a small portion of what God has entrusted to us, and these funds are used to fulfill the Great Commission. What an incredible demonstration of God's grace! He commands us to give for the purpose of displaying His mercy and building His kingdom, and then He gives us the money with which to obey. The fact that the government uses some of our tax money to meet the needs of the poor is irrelevant to our responsibility to tithe – we would never consider the government's use of our tax dollars to repay _its_ debt an exemption from our biblical responsibility to repay our own debts!

DISCOVER

Read 2 Corinthians 9:6. How might this verse apply to the Christian who tithes on their net income vs. their gross income?

_____

_____

_____

_____

Whether tithing on grain, flocks, or financial resources, the first and best portion is reserved for the Lord. If we were to tithe on our net income, we would actually be placing the government above God in that the first part of our income would be given to pay taxes, with God receiving His portion from the leftovers. Only by tithing on our gross income does God receive the firstfruits, and that is the portion that He has called us to return.

Where to Give

Another question that is frequently raised concerning giving involves where, or to whom, we are to give. Specifically, many Christians wonder whether the entire tithe is to be given to the local church, or if it is acceptable to give part of the tithe to individuals in need, other ministries, missionaries, etc. Once we've acknowledged God's call for us to give, and we understand the three different levels of giving (tithe, freewill offerings, and sacrificial giving), the next step is to answer the question, "To whom do we give?"

It is commonly taught that, whereas we have complete freedom in deciding where to give our freewill offerings, the whole tithe is to be given to the local church (i.e., the church that you regularly attend or of which you are a member). Although this is the decision that my wife and I have made, I would humbly disagree with the position that it is a biblical mandate.

DISCOVER

Read Malachi 3:10. Where does God instruct Israel to give their tithe? What do you think this means?

_____

_____

_____

This passage of scripture is frequently cited to support the position of giving the entire tithe to the local church. In this case the "storehouse" is equated with the local church, and we are taught that obedience in tithing involves giving at least 10 percent of our gross income to our local church fellowship.

REFLECT

How many churches were there in the Old Testament?

_____

How many churches are there in the New Testament? (Hint: See Ephesians 5:23 and Colossians 1:18,24.)

_____

The answer to both questions is the same: one. Many Christians today tend to think that there are as many different churches as there are buildings with a steeple and cross on the top. This view is exacerbated by the existence of so many denominations, most of which convey a less-than-unified attitude toward one another. We don't think that there is only one church because our local churches tend to function as distinctly separate entities from other churches in the same town. But the Bible teaches that there is only one church, the body of Christ, of which Jesus is the Head.

I have no problem with a Christian's personal conviction to give their entire tithe to the local church. I do have a problem, however, with the teaching that each local church is a separate "storehouse" to which each member is bound to give 10 percent. If your tithe is going to Christ's work, whether through one organization or many, you are obeying God and bringing the whole tithe into the storehouse.

DISCOVER

Read Matthew 28:19. In this passage Jesus summarizes the primary work of the church. What is it?

_____

_____

What role does our giving play in fulfilling this calling?

_____

_____

I've often been asked how a person makes the decision as to what part of their giving should go to their local church. My first answer is to ask God. *"If any of you lacks wisdom, he should ask God,"* we're told in James 1:5, *"who gives generously to all without finding fault, **and it will be given to him"*** (emphasis mine). James goes on to remind us that we must ask in faith, believing and not doubting. What a glorious promise! I have this verse framed and hanging in my office, a daily reminder as to the Source of all wisdom, and God's promise to provide it when I ask. The next step in this decision-making process involves the principle of accountability, and that is the basis of much of the individual counsel I've given on this subject.

REFLECT

Why might accountability be an important factor in deciding whether or not to support a particular ministry?

_____

_____

An example of the principle of accountability in giving can be found in Paul's letters to the church at Corinth. As a brief background, in Acts 11:28 a prophet named Agabus predicted a severe famine that would impact the entire Roman Empire. This famine struck prior to 54 A.D., during the reign of Claudius, emperor of Rome, and it devastated the church in Jerusalem. As a result, during his missionary journeys Paul would encourage generous gifts from the churches in each area to assist the famine-stricken Christians in Jerusalem. In his first letter to the church at Corinth, written around 55 A.D., Paul had given specific instructions concerning their gifts.

DISCOVER

Read 1 Corinthians 16:1-2. How did Paul suggest the church collect funds for the brothers in Jerusalem?

_____

_____

How is this method similar to what is practiced in the church today?

_____

_____

This scenario is followed up in 2 Corinthians 8. Paul notes that he is sending his associate, Titus, back to the church in Corinth to encourage them to complete the generous giving to which they had committed, but which had apparently stalled. Titus was sent because, not only had he organized the collection when it was started a year earlier, but he also had established a relationship of love, trust, and affection with the church at Corinth. (See 2 Corinthians 7:6-7, 13-15.)

DISCOVER

Read 2 Corinthians 8:16-22. When Titus returned to Corinth, how many other men were sent to accompany him (see verses 18 and 22)?

_____

_____

_____

How were these men described by Paul?

_____

_____

_____

In addition to Paul and Titus, two other men, both well known and trusted by the church, were mentioned as being selected to collect and distribute these generous offerings to the suffering families in Jerusalem. Although the identities of these two men were not specified, two logical candidates are Barnabas and Luke, both of whom traveled with Paul and were known for their faithfulness in ministry.

REFLECT

Who is the most trustworthy person you know?

_____

What is it about their character that makes them trustworthy?

_____

_____

Imagine that one Sunday you are unable to attend worship, so you give your weekly offering to your trustworthy friend and ask him or her to put it in the offering plate for you. Do you have any doubt that it will arrive safely at its intended destination? Would you ask your friend to take along several honorable witnesses to make sure the gift is delivered? Such a concern would probably never enter your mind, and I'm not sure it would have occurred to the Corinthian church either. Paul was directly responsible for planting many of the new churches, and he was deeply loved and respected by most of the Christians in those areas.

It is doubtful that the church at Corinth would have objected to Paul's collecting the gift himself and promising to deliver it. Still, Paul insisted on sending along with Titus two trustworthy men, and the three of them would accompany Paul as he delivered these gifts to the church at Jerusalem. Paul believed in absolute accountability with regard to administering the gifts of God's people.

DISCOVER

Read 2 Corinthians 8:20-21. What two reasons did Paul give for the way he was handling these gifts?

1. _____

2. _____

This passage is extremely helpful and instructive, especially in seeking God's wisdom about allocating our tithes and offerings. When folks ask me how much of their giving should go to the local church as opposed to other ministry needs, I ask several important questions. You might find it helpful to answer these questions about your own church.

1. Is your church exercising wise stewardship over
   the funds entrusted to them?   ❏ Yes ❏ No

2. Is the annual budget given to the congregation?   ❏ Yes ❏ No

3. Are you comfortable with the integrity of your
   leaders/officers?   ❏ Yes ❏ No

4. Are there appropriate checks and balances in
   the handling of funds?   ❏ Yes ❏ No

5. Has the church been effective in its ministry?   ❏ Yes ❏ No

6. Do you support the church's mission and vision?   ❏ Yes ❏ No

7. Do you have any concerns regarding the
   handling of the church's financial resources?   ❏ Yes ❏ No

Incidentally, these same questions should be asked of *every* ministry for which you are considering financial support.

In the case of my own family, we are highly committed to the mission statement of our church, and we have a great deal of trust in the integrity of our pastors and officers. I'm very comfortable with how the funds are physically handled, and I believe the Lord has been using us increasingly to impact our community for the cause of Christ. For these reasons, and having prayerfully sought the Lord's promised wisdom many years ago, we have made a commitment to give at least 10 percent of our gross income to our church. That is our own personal conviction.

There have been cases, however, in which I've counseled families to give less than a tithe to their church and, in a few isolated instances, not to give there at all. In the latter cases, as you might imagine, this counsel was quickly followed by a suggestion that they find another church.

Give an example of a case in which it would be necessary for a Christian to withhold financial support from a ministry.

_____

_____

_____

Imagine that you are a member of a church in which there appear to be serious problems of integrity concerning the handling of church funds, with a decreasing level of openness and accountability among church leaders. It is becoming increasingly difficult for church members to get answers to questions about how the money is being spent. Long-standing policies are starting to be violated, and several faithful families, frustrated in their efforts to resolve these issues, have left the church. In this situation, your interest is not simply in understanding general biblical guidelines on how much a Christian should give to the local church; you want desperately to understand how much of *your* giving should go to *this* particular church, in these particular circumstances.

Let's assume you have always given at least 10 percent to your church, but now you instinctively sense that continuing to do so would no longer represent good stewardship of the resources the Lord had entrusted to you. You are not struggling with guilt over not giving enough, but rather that you are giving at all. You can't say for certain that there is illegality involved, but there is certainly a strong appearance of impropriety and those involved refuse to be confronted or held accountable. In this case, I would most likely advise you to continue giving your tithes and offerings, but to give the funds to ministries other than this church. If the problems persist, it might be time to find another church.

REFLECT

Have you ever stopped giving to a ministry that you had been supporting?

_____

_____

If so, what circumstances led to your decision?

_____

_____

All giving, whether to the local church or other ministries, must be done prayerfully and purposefully, using the wisdom that God provides and the guidelines laid out in His Word. We should never allow our consciences to be bound by teaching that suggests that the first 10 percent of our income must, in all circumstances, be given to the local church, regardless of how well the church manages these resources. Godly wisdom and our own sanctified common sense must be brought to bear in all giving decisions.

Our next example involves a Christian who has great passion for foreign missions. She has frequently been involved in short-term missions trips overseas and provides financial support for quite a number of missionaries with whom she has developed relationships over the years. This woman loves her local church and strongly supports its ministry plan. The church's vision has much more emphasis on local (as opposed to foreign) missions, with a focus on outreach and evangelism in its own community.

Let's assume this faithful Christian is giving a total of 12 percent of her gross income to God's work. If she were to give the first 10 percent to her local church, there would be very little left to give to the area of ministry that represents her greatest passion. Both of these works (local and foreign missions) are part of the Great Commission, to which all Christians are called. Neither is more or less important than the other. It is certainly acceptable for this generous giver to divide her tithe between the local church and her foreign missions involvement. All of the funds are flowing into the same storehouse.

REFLECT

What area(s) of ministry are you most passionate about?

_____

_____

_____

To what extent does your current giving reflect your interest in that area of ministry?

_____

_____

_____

Giving vs. Debt Repayment

Another important issue I want to address is the common, but flawed, paradigm I've given in the heading. Most of us have some level of debt, whether it be a mortgage, a car loan, student loans, or credit cards. Statistics also indicate that most Christians do not tithe. The excuse that is often given for not tithing goes something like this: "Money is tight each month and I have a lot of debt. God commands us to repay our debts. If I start tithing I will have to cut back on the amount of my debt repayment." This argument is sometimes further justified with their often hollow promise: "After I get out of debt, I'll be able to tithe."

The flaw in this reasoning is that we have to choose between giving and repaying our debts. The Bible knows of no such conflict. God's command to give to His work is not conditional. The Lord doesn't instruct us to "tithe if you're debt-free," "tithe if your budget allows," or "tithe if there are funds left over after making the maximum contribution to your 401K plan." Repaying our debts, budgeting, and saving for retirement are all good things, but they have nothing to do with our responsibility to give generously.

REFLECT

Has this flawed paradigm had an impact on the way you think about tithing? If so, in what way?

_____

_____

_____

_____

_____

We must resist the temptation to create an unbiblical hierarchy for the allocation of our income. Financial author Ron Blue, in his excellent book *Master Your Money,* lays out for us the five uses of money that are commanded in the Scriptures: giving, taxes, debt repayment, living expenses, and saving.[1] All five areas are biblical, practical, and necessary. When I studied the biblical references to these areas I quickly noticed a striking point: *All are treated with equal importance.* Consider the following examples.

God commands us to provide for the needs of our families. But we're never instructed to choose between this priority and paying our taxes. Similarly, we're told that saving is wise, but it is not treated as being more important than repaying our debts. This one may come as a surprise, especially in view of how strongly I've urged you to consider tithing, but giving is not a priority over saving, paying our taxes, debt repayment, or providing for the physical needs of our families. All are important, and all are of equal priority. Tithing comes first chronologically, but that doesn't in any way minimize or negate our God-given responsibility to the other areas.

REFLECT

Give an example of how a Christian could be giving away 15 percent of his income but failing to honor God in other areas.

_____

_____

_____

_____

_____

My experience is that this concept comes as a shock to most Christians. I've noticed the disbelieving look in people's eyes as I've counseled them to use part of their unexpected bonus check to take a family vacation. It's as if I was expected to counsel them that, if they wanted to be really spiritual, they should give it all away. Obviously, I have nothing against giving generously, and at times, sacrificially. But God does not instruct us to neglect the other areas of financial responsibility in order to give more money away. God doesn't need our money — He already owns everything. Managing money in accordance with God's principles involves prudently balancing all of these priorities. They are not mutually exclusive.

REFLECT

What is your reaction to the concept that giving, saving, living expenses, debt repayment, and paying our taxes are all commanded by God and are of equal priority?

_____

_____

_____

_____

"Non-monetary" Tithing

Another popular issue in the discussion on biblical giving concerns what I call "non-monetary" tithing. Perhaps you have heard someone refer to the practice of "tithing my time," and it simply refers to consciously giving 10 percent of your work time or free time to kingdom work. This could take the form of a person volunteering at a local soup kitchen or crisis pregnancy center, or it might involve an attorney making sure that a portion of the cases he or she accepts are pro bono. Some folks will coach sports in a high-risk urban area while others will do short-term mission work overseas. Non-monetary tithing is simply a way of recognizing that God, in addition to giving us money and material possessions, has likewise given us time and abilities. One way of acknowledging God's provision in these areas is to give freely of your time and talents to serve others in the Lord's name.

REFLECT

Share a ministry example from your life that could be classified as tithing your possessions, time, or talents.

_____

_____

_____

_____

Who could possibly fault this idea? Let me begin by saying that this idea is laudable, biblical, honorable, and wonderful. Our Savior modeled for us a life of compassionate service, and then He instructed us to *"go and do likewise"* (Luke 10:37). So, what's my concern? The only problem I've found in this practice is when it is used as a *substitute* for the monetary tithe.

Almost every class I teach on this subject will involve someone's sharing with the group that, although they can't give 10 percent of their income to the Lord's work, they make up for it by tithing their time. This is where I struggle. Obviously, there is nothing wrong with giving our time and talent in service to the Lord, but that has absolutely nothing to do with our responsibility to give financially as well. Frankly, for many of us, we would much rather give away some our time, regardless of how busy we are, than to give our money. God calls us to both — it is not an either/or proposition.

REFLECT

Which is easier for you to give away, time or money? Why?

_____

_____

_____

_____

Most folks who take the position that it is okay to tithe time instead of money do not bother trying to justify it biblically. The only such attempt I occasionally hear is a reference to the parable of the talents in Matthew 25, with the insistence that the word *talent* represents our God-given ability (as opposed to money). The text itself dispels this myth:

> *"Again, it will be like a man going on a journey, who called his servants and entrusted his property to them. To one he gave five talents **of money**, to another two talents, and to another one talent, each according to his ability"*
>
> —Matthew 25:14-15, emphasis mine

This term is similarly used elsewhere in the Bible.

DISCOVER
Read 1 Kings 20:39. To what does the term *talent* refer in this passage?

_____

_____

_____

_____

Let me summarize by saying that I would encourage us in the strongest terms to joyfully give of our time and talents. But let's not mock God's Word by assuming that this activity fulfills His call to tithe on the income that He so faithfully provides.

Is It Ever Okay *Not* to Tithe?

This is an interesting question, and one on which there is not a clear consensus in the church. The framework within which we should address this issue is two-fold: First, I believe that God calls all of His people to give at least a tithe, and second, tithing is not a form of legalism. Remember that God doesn't need our money — we've seen that He owns everything. Our obedient giving is for our own benefit. If you don't believe it, ask someone who is a generous giver. They derive far greater blessing from the money they give away than they do from the money they save or spend. When we invest in God's work, the benefits and blessings are temporal as well as eternal. The Gospel is being proclaimed in your own neighborhood and to the far reaches of the globe, all funded by the tithes and offerings of God's people. The poor are being clothed and fed, the sick are being cared for, the imprisoned are being visited and led to faith in Jesus Christ, all because Christians throughout the world have the privilege of giving to kingdom work!

That is why tithing is not a form of legalism. If it becomes so, we should keep our money in our pockets because *legalistic giving does not honor God.*

DISCOVER

Read Matthew 10:8 and 2 Corinthians 9:7. What words are used to describe how we are to give?

1. _____ 2. _____

What words are used to describe how we are *not* to give?

1. _____ 2. _____

The Greek word for *cheerful* can also be translated as "hilarious."[2] What does a hilarious giver look like? A lot different, I suspect, than a legalistic giver. Giving that is honoring to God is both obedient and joyful. We don't give out of obligation, but because we have been given the privilege to do so.

Our attitude is to be like that of the Macedonian church which, the apostle Paul notes, *"urgently pleaded with us for the privilege of sharing in this service to the saints"* (2 Corinthians 8:4). Imagine that...a local church pleading with their favorite missionary to have the privilege of giving to his ministry. (I know a number of missionaries that would love to experience that problem!) Note also that the church at Macedonia was very poor, yet they wouldn't be denied the opportunity to share in Paul's ministry of church planting and evangelism. Although it is certainly true that their giving was a demonstration of their faithfulness and obedience to God, their gifts were clearly not given legalistically. They gave generously, joyfully, even hilariously. That should be our model.

REFLECT

Give an example of a financial gift that you've given that was accompanied by a great sense of joy.

_____

_____

_____

What does all of this have to do with the question, "Is it ever okay not to tithe?" I wanted to begin with this framework because I understand how our sinful flesh operates. When we ask this particular question, it is not usually because we're unable to tithe, but because we're looking for a way to avoid doing so. I can't help us there; believe me, I spent a significant amount of time trying to disprove this principle so I could keep using that income to support my inflated lifestyle. The bottom line, I am absolutely persuaded from the Scriptures, is that we are all called to give back to God from the firstfruits of our income, and this giving for all of us starts with a tithe.

In order to more directly answer this important question, however, I must ask us to define the word *okay*. Is it okay not to spend time in God's Word? Is it okay not to attend church? Is it okay not to participate in the sacrament of the Lord's Supper? Well, yes and no. From an eternal perspective, I would have to say all of these decisions would be "okay." For folks who have trusted in Jesus Christ for the forgiveness of their sins and the promise of eternal life in heaven, failing to do these things will have no eternal consequence. That is to say their sins are indeed forgiven, and they will most assuredly spend eternity in heaven. However, these actions are not without temporal consequences.

DISCOVER

Write out 1 Corinthians 10:23 and consider it as you continue reading.

_____

_____

_____

_____

_____

We are instructed in the scriptures to participate in all of the following: the tithe (Matthew 23:23 and 1 Corinthians 16:1-5); worship (Psalm 100:2; Hebrews 10:25; and John 4:23-24); and the Lord's Supper (1 Corinthians 11:23-26). The instructions God gives us are for our own good. It is "okay" not to do these things in the sense that our eternal security is not jeopardized by our disobedience. I would propose, however, that it is foolish to purposely violate the clear instruction from our loving Father who knows what is best for us. In that sense, it is certainly not "okay" to ignore these important practices.

My heavenly Father will not suffer, nor will His plans be thwarted, because I in my disobedience fail to tithe, attend worship, or participate in the Lord's Supper. It is I who will suffer from my neglect, first by missing out on the many temporal blessings that obedience will bring, and second by experiencing the chastisement that my Father might lovingly bestow, *"because the LORD disciplines those He loves"* (Proverbs 3:12). Is it ever "okay" not to tithe? I would have to concur with Paul's words in 1 Corinthians 10:23: *"Everything is permissible"* — *but not everything is beneficial.* Failing to tithe may, at times be permissible, but I don't believe it is ever beneficial.

REFLECT

Give a practical example of something that is permissible for you but is clearly not beneficial.

_____

_____

_____

_____

What about the new Christian who was already struggling financially before ever learning about God's calling to tithe? Or the single mom who barely has enough each month to make ends meet? Or the dad who lost his job and temporarily has to make due with his meager unemployment checks? How can these folks afford to tithe? Thankfully, in such cases as in all of Christian life, there is grace. There are times when the Christian's faith is brand new, weak, or badly shaken. In such cases it can be very difficult to give generously. If I were asked for my counsel in each of these cases, however, I would strongly encourage a commitment to giving at some level. Allow me to explain.

DISCOVER

Read 2 Corinthians 9:7a. What amount was Paul suggesting be given in this passage?

_____

_____

_____

_____

Remember that giving is a demonstration, not only of obedience, but also of faith. The more challenging our current financial circumstances, the more desperately we need to rely on our Father's extraordinary provision. We prove our dependence, as well as our trust, by giving to the Lord's work even when we don't understand how we can possibly afford it. God owns *the cattle on a thousand hills* (Psalm 50:10); whom better to appeal to when we are struggling financially?

I like to use an illustration when I teach on this subject. Pointing to a blackboard, I'll ask the class to imagine that all of the material possessions of the universe, all of which belong to God, are contained within the surface of the blackboard. Then I'll ask someone to draw a circle representing the proportionate amount of all God's money and possessions that He has entrusted to their personal care. Even a very wealthy person would have to acknowledge that they are in "control" of only a tiny fraction of the Lord's total belongings. Most of us couldn't draw a circle small enough! Then I'll ask, "When financial difficulty arises, which group of possessions would you rather have access to: God's or your own?" The point is that when we obediently and faithfully give back to God just a portion of what He entrusts to us, we open ourselves to benefit from His limitless resources during our time of need. God promises to bless our giving, and He is always faithful to provide for the needs of His children.

DISCOVER

Read Psalm 37:25 and Philippians 4:19. What do these passages teach about God's provision for His people?

_____

_____

_____

_____

The Next Step

So you can't afford to give? You're going through a painful and difficult financial trial? *"Test me in this,"* our Creator challenges us in Malachi 3, *"and see if I will not throw open the floodgates of heaven, and pour out so much blessing that you will not have room enough for it"* (verse 10). The question during financial trials is not, "Can I afford to tithe?" but rather, "Can I afford *not* to tithe?"

I'm reminded of a difficult time that my family went through after a career change that resulted in a significantly reduced income. Lori was pregnant with our fourth child and had become somewhat concerned about the cost of clothing the new baby. A couple of years earlier we had given away all of our baby clothes and toys to other families in need. Now it was we who were expecting again, and with finances already tight, the cost of a new family member caused some concern.

I remember that Lori was, for some reason, particularly fixated on baby shoes. We had given away many pairs, and as you can certainly attest if you have children, new baby shoes have a very short life and are very expensive. I don't know why Lori was so focused in her financial concerns about this particular item, but she constantly talked about the difficulty of affording the shoes for our baby. As if to demonstrate both His gracious provision and His sense of humor, God provided so many free pairs of baby shoes for this child that an entire shelf in our bedroom was covered with them. We had committed to continue our practice of tithing during what had become the most difficult time of our lives financially, and God once again demonstrated His faithfulness by providing for all of our needs. *"Whoever sows sparingly will also reap sparingly, and whoever sows generously will also reap generously"* (2 Corinthians 9:6).

REFLECT

Describe an experience in which you have witnessed God's extraordinary provision during a time of need.

_____

_____

_____

_____

_____

_____

If you are convicted about tithing but your finances seem beyond repair and your monthly bills exceed your normal income, try this: Go to the Lord in prayer. Tell Him you believe that He calls all of His people to tithe but that you don't understand how it can possibly work in your case. Commit to giving some amount of your monthly income immediately, as a demonstration of your belief that God alone can provide for your needs. Ask Him to increase your faith.

As you pray, commit to a certain time frame within which you will work your way up to a tithe, and then begin your giving with whatever amount you have committed to the Lord. Test God! Begin right where you are to believe His glorious promises. Then, once you've committed to begin giving some amount regularly, follow through on this commitment no matter how difficult it seems. Take the apostle Paul's advice: *"Now finish the work, so that your eager willingness to do it may be matched by your completion of it, according to your means"* (2 Corinthians 8:11). At this stage in your walk with the Lord, the amount is considerably less important than the faith and obedience you are demonstrating. Even this seemingly modest step will lead you to a greater understanding of God's immense love for you, His commitment to you, and His ability to provide for all of your needs.

COMMIT

If you don't already have a consistent giving plan in place, spend time this week in prayer asking the Lord to lead you in developing one. Then make a prayerful and firm commitment to follow through with this plan.

Summary

Whether you are going through financial struggles or find yourself with excess resources, God encourages you to give generously. We live in the wealthiest nation in the world, and yet every year ministries close and missionaries leave the field for lack of adequate funding. The problem is not that there aren't enough resources in the hands of Christians to do the work that God has called us to do; the problem is that we cling to the resources He has entrusted to us. That is why I've always believed that financial freedom is never a function of how much we have; rather, it is a function of how much we give away. To give freely and generously is to experience true freedom. To desperately cling to money and possessions despite the need around us is just another form of financial bondage. These chains are broken as we increase our giving — not because we have to, but because we truly want to give to God's kingdom.

STUDY QUESTIONS

1. How would you respond if a fellow Christian asked if they should be tithing on their gross or their net income?

_____

_____

_____

2. Under what circumstances would a Christian be justified in not giving any portion of his tithe to his local church?

_____

_____

_____

3. What counsel would you give to a fellow Christian who decided to wait until all of their debts were paid off before they began tithing?

_____

_____

_____

4. Give an example of non-monetary tithing. Should this practice be substituted for tithing our income?

_____

_____

_____

5. How would you answer the question, "Is it ever okay not to tithe?"

_____

_____

_____

6. What principle that you learned in this chapter was most helpful?

_____

_____

_____

-6-
SETTING GOALS
PART 1

"Woe to those who go to great depths to hide their plans from the LORD, who do their work in darkness and think, 'Who sees us? Who will know?'"
—The Prophet Isaiah, Isaiah 29:15

"Commit to the LORD whatever you do, and your plans will succeed."
—King Solomon, Proverbs 16:3

Before I became a Christian I was obsessive about setting goals. Since my "god" was money and possessions, most of my goals naturally fell into these two categories. That was the baggage I brought into my initial study of biblical financial principles. Since my history with this practice involved setting goals apart from God, and pursuing material things instead of God, I was most reluctant as a new Christian to set goals at all. It felt sinful to do so, and every time I contemplated a new set of objectives, I became concerned that I was slipping back into my former way of thinking.

REFLECT
What is your current attitude toward setting goals? •

_____

_____

_____

_____

_____

As I studied God's Word it became increasingly clear that God calls us to plan and to set goals. I realized that it wasn't the process of setting goals that was dishonoring to the Lord; it was my sinful and selfish motivation.

DISCOVER

Read Proverbs 21:2. What does this passage teach about setting goals?

_____

_____

_____

_____

One potential argument against the process of planning and goal setting is the following passage in James 4:

> _Now listen, you who say, "Today or tomorrow we will go to this or that city, spend a year there, carry on business and make money." Why, you do not even know what will happen tomorrow. What is your life? You are a mist that appears for a little while and then vanishes._
>
> —Verses 13-14

If you are familiar with this passage, you'll remember that verse 15 brings some clarification, which I'll address later. But folks who aren't inclined to set goals will point to this passage as proof that such planning is futile. "Why plan for tomorrow? We don't even know if we'll be here." The position seems to be reinforced by verse 16, which states that _as it is, you boast and brag. All such boasting is evil._ I struggled with this passage for some time, thinking that goal setting was a sinful part of my former life which had no place in God's economy.

REFLECT

What "baggage," if any, do you bring to the process of setting goals?

_____

_____

_____

A closer examination of this passage, particularly verse 15, drives home the point that James is intending to make: _Instead, you ought to say, "If it is the Lord's will, we will live and do this or that."_ It took me some time to understand that what is being condemned here is not the process of planning, but rather planning _apart from God._

If I'm setting goals for myself or my family without consulting God, particularly through His Word and prayer, I am choosing to go my own way and should not expect to be blessed. I am "boasting" in the sense that I'm claiming my independence, that I can do this myself and have no need of God. Not only is this type of planning sinful, it is foolish.

God's people have a history of such disobedience: *We all, like sheep, have gone astray, each of us has turned to his own way* (Isaiah 53:6). Israel chose to go her own way, and the result was forty years of wandering in the desert before finally being allowed to enter the Promised Land. Their subsequent choices of independence from God resulted in seventy years of captivity in Babylon. Are we any different?

God has given us clear guidelines for the handling of those resources He has entrusted to us. Still, we are prone to ignore His teaching, preferring instead to use His money for our own selfish ends. As a result, we find ourselves wandering in a financial desert, experiencing our own version of fiscal captivity. Far from teaching that planning and setting goals is wrong, the Bible consistently reinforces the importance of doing so.

DISCOVER

What does each of the following passages teach us about our plans and goals?

Proverbs 16:9

_____

_____

Proverbs 21:5

_____

_____

Proverbs 14:15

_____

_____

Proverbs 16:3

_____

_____

Psalm 32:8

_____

_____

Luke 14:28

_____

_____

God Has a Plan

God's plan for Adam was to tend the garden, to take dominion, and to be fruitful and multiply. His plan for Noah was to build the ark. Abraham was to become a great nation, through whom all the nations of the world would be blessed. Joseph was entrusted with developing the plan that kept God's people from becoming extinct when a severe famine hit. Moses was called to lead God's people out of slavery in Egypt. Joshua led the conquest into the Promised Land.

REFLECT

Have you ever considered that God might have specific plans for your life? Why or why not?

_____

_____

_____

The list goes on. David was to be King of Israel; Solomon was to build the temple; Jonah was sent to call the people of Nineveh to repentance. John the Baptist prepared the way for the coming Messiah, and the Virgin Mary was called to carry Him to His birth. Jesus, I rejoice to report to those hearing this for the first time, came to save His people from their sins and grant them eternal life!

Peter and the apostles were sent to preach the Good News to the Jewish people, and the apostle Paul was set apart from birth as a preacher to the Gentiles. Stephen was to be the first martyr, and Luke was called to write one of the four Gospels. God's Word is replete with examples of particular goals that He had for particular people. God's part was to call each person to a specific task; their job was to obediently follow God's will, wherever it led. For every example I just cited we could easily find a lesser known, seemingly obscure man and woman, who figured no less prominently in God's plan for redemptive history.

DISCOVER

Read 1 Kings 7:13-14. What was God's specific plan for Huram, and how had God prepared him for this calling?

_____

_____

_____

_____

What Is a Goal?

Webster's Collegiate Dictionary defines the word *goal* as "an object or end that one strives to attain."[1] I think that works as a generic definition, but it might not help us in seeking to set goals that are honoring to God and consistent with His principles and directives. I prefer to think of a goal as *"one aspect of God's plan for my life."* Some goals are relatively easy to discern because they are clearly spelled out in God's Word and have general application to all of us.

REFLECT

Give two examples of general goals that apply to all of God's people.

1. _____

2. _____

I know, for example, that it is God's will for me to remain faithful to my wife. It is His will for me to give back to Him a portion of the income He entrusts to me. It is

His plan for me to *"go and make disciples"* (Matthew 28:19). These are examples of general goals that are revealed in the Scriptures and that apply to all of us, both collectively and individually. The struggle for most of us, however, has to do with God's *specific* plans for each of us as individuals. For example, I might seek God's direction for which job I should take, where I should live, or who I should marry. That is where goal setting becomes a bit more challenging. I will devote the next chapter to this particular issue, providing detailed instructions for discovering the specific plans that God has for our lives.

Goal-Setting Tips

Before we begin the process of setting personal financial goals that are honoring to God, let's turn our attention to four important foundational principles that are the starting point for such planning.

1. SPEND TIME WITH THE LORD. We have discussed the importance of seeking the Lord during the process of making plans and setting goals. Do not attempt to do this apart from the Lord. Otherwise, you might end up like so many folks who are relentlessly pursuing things that are inconsistent with God's plan for their lives.

DISCOVER

Read Proverbs 21:30. What does this passage teach us about planning?

_____

_____

_____

_____

_____

Search the Scriptures and spend time in prayer, asking the Lord to direct your thoughts and desires. It is a joyful thing indeed to experience the Lord's leading as He faithfully answers your prayers for wisdom.

Read Psalm 32:8. How does this passage encourage us concerning God's involvement in our planning process?

_____

_____

_____

2. DO NOT BE DISCOURAGED BY THE PAST. Our past experiences can either be a help or a hindrance to us. If you've set a few goals in the past and actually achieved them, you won't be intimidated by setting new goals for your finances. If you've had the opposite experience, never completing a goal that was set, there's a chance that you might resist trying again.

REFLECT

Share a past experience with setting goals that might positively or negatively impact your willingness to set new goals in the future.

_____

_____

_____

As we continue in this discussion about setting financial goals, I want to encourage you to move forward regardless of what you may have been through in the past. All of us have tried and failed, and sometimes we've been humiliated in the process. Avoid dragging such baggage into this process. This is a time to look ahead, not back.

DISCOVER

Read Isaiah 43:18-19. What point is God making that can encourage us as we set personal financial goals?

_____

_____

_____

_____

3. DO NOT LIMIT GOD. As you begin to search the Scriptures and pray, you might sense God's leading to set a goal that doesn't seem achievable from a human perspective. For example, I once counseled a family that had an extremely high amount of consumer debt. As you can imagine, this debt was causing tremendous stress and limited their ability to give or save. As we talked and prayed, the overwhelming sense was that God was calling them to begin immediately to work on repaying all of their debt. This truly seemed impossible because they already had a significant negative cash flow. Convicted, however, they committed to this goal and began to pray fervently for God's intervention.

The next several months included an extraordinary turn of events. They both increased their hours at work to improve their cash flow, and they sold a vehicle we agreed they could no longer afford to keep. They also started tithing, having no idea how they could make it work but convinced that this was part of God's plan. We then watched in joyful amazement as the Lord intervened in an incredible way. This couple did everything they could think of to do, and they trusted God to do those things that only He could do. Within a year, they called me back to report that they were completely debt-free! One part of God's specific plan for their lives had been faithfully sought and executed.

Your Father in heaven owns all of the silver and gold (Haggai 2:8) and the cattle on a thousand hills (Psalm 50:10). He delights to use His limitless resources to help His children who faithfully move forward when He gives the instruction. Do not limit God!

DISCOVER

Read Ephesians 3:20. What does this passage teach us about God's ability to provide?

_____

_____

_____

_____

4. COMMIT YOUR GOALS TO THE LORD. After you've spent time in God's Word and in prayer, and have arrived at a list of specific financial goals that you think the Lord has directed, there are two great reasons to commit these plans to the Lord *before* taking action. First, it is a great way to double check your motivation. Remember that the flesh can be deceiving. It is important to go continually before the Lord asking Him to affirm His direction.

I remember a counseling situation many years ago in which a friend was seeking God's leading in how to reduce debt and begin to save regularly. These goals were very consistent with biblical principles. While pursuing these specific goals, however, a severe lack of contentment quickly set in. The next time I saw my friend he was driving a new car. Not only was the new loan amount considerably larger than the old loan, the loss on the old car — which had been running just fine, by the way — had been rolled into the new loan. The result of this transaction: Total debt had increased and cash flow worsened.

Sometimes we start out by seeking God's leading, but then we get tired of waiting and take matters into our own hands. It is always easy for us to say "God led me to do this," but God doesn't provide direction that violates His own principles. In the case I just described, the goal to buy a new car could not possibly have come from the Lord. Had this idea been committed back to God before action was taken, I believe there would have been a strong sense of conviction that it was a mistake. The first reason, then, that we commit our goals to the Lord is to make sure we haven't deceived ourselves somewhere along the way in the planning process.

REFLECT

Share a personal experience in which you made a significant financial decision that was most likely not a part of God's plan for you.

_____

_____

_____

The second reason we commit each specific goal to the Lord is because we seek His intervention. Goal setting is not about what we can do; it is about what God will do through us. By continually going back to the Lord and praying about our particular goals, we are not only asking for His help in achieving them, but we are reminding ourselves of our absolute dependence on Him. When He blesses us by allowing a goal to be accomplished, we are able to give God the glory because we know it is His doing.

DISCOVER

Read Proverbs 16:3. What does this verse teach us about setting goals?

_____

_____

_____

REJOICE

Pause for a moment to consider the perfect, personal love that your heavenly Father has for you. The almighty God, who created and sustains the entire universe, is so intimately involved in your life that He promises, "I will instruct you and teach you in the way you should go; I will counsel you and watch over you" (Psalm 32:8). Rejoice and praise God for His direct involvement in your life!

Now that we've looked at some basic principles that will help you set goals that are honoring to the Lord, let's begin to move from the general to the specific. In the next chapter we'll discuss the four steps involved in the process of discerning God's will for specific areas and decisions in your life.

STUDY QUESTIONS

1. How did you feel about setting financial goals before you began this study?

_____

_____

_____

_____

2. What type of planning is condemned in James 4:13-16?

_____

_____

_____

_____

3. How might we define the term *goal* as it relates to God's plan?

_____

_____

_____

_____

4. What is the first step in preparing to set personal financial goals?

_____

_____

_____

_____

5. What are the two reasons that it is wise to commit our goals to the Lord?

_____

_____

_____

_____

6. How has your thinking about setting goals been impacted by the information presented in this chapter?

_____

_____

_____

_____

-7-
SETTING GOALS
PART 2

The LORD Almighty has sworn, "Surely, as I have planned, so it will be, and as I have purposed, so it will stand."

—The Prophet Isaiah, Isaiah 14:24

"For I know the plans I have for you," declares the LORD, "plans to prosper you and not to harm you, plans to give you hope and a future."

—The Prophet Jeremiah, Jeremiah 29:11

As we discussed in the previous chapter, the greatest challenge most Christians face in setting personal goals is discerning God's will. We acknowledge that His Word provides clear instructions for our lives in general, especially in the areas of morality and living out our faith. These instructions apply very broadly to all of us, and they are relatively easy to discern. I don't have to wonder whether or not God wants me to cheat on my taxes or worship idols because He has directly addressed such issues in the Bible.

The challenge comes, however, when I must choose a place to live or decide which job to take. Should I pursue marriage or remain single? Should we try to have children, adopt, or remain childless? Each day we are faced with important decisions, most of which are morally neutral and are not specifically addressed in the Scriptures. How should we go about making such decisions?

REFLECT

Share an example of a major decision you have struggled with recently. How did you feel about your understanding of God's will for that particular decision?

_____

_____

_____

Discerning God's Will

There are four important steps that I recommend in seeking to discern God's will in your particular circumstances. I was blessed to receive this instruction early in my Christian life, and it has proven to be invaluable as I've sought to walk in accordance with God's plan for my life. I will present these steps in order of importance and priority.

1. GOD'S WORD – Without question, the most important step in the process of discerning God's will, both in matters general and specific, is knowing God's Word. We desire to make plans and set goals that are honoring to God. In order to know what He desires for us, to do what pleases Him, and avoid dishonoring Him, we must spend time reading the Bible.

DISCOVER
Write out Psalm 119:9-10.

_____

_____

_____

Knowing God's Word not only helps us determine the types of goals that are appropriate, it also helps us discern those that are wrongly motivated. An example of an appropriate goal is demonstrated in Acts 1:15-26. This passage takes place just after Jesus had ascended into heaven, when the apostles returned to Jerusalem just prior to Pentecost. Peter began to exercise his leadership by suggesting that they choose a man to replace Judas Iscariot, who had betrayed Christ and subsequently killed himself. There had been twelve apostles but now there were eleven, and Peter had determined that the first course of action was to replace Judas.

What motivated Peter to set this particular objective? It was his knowledge of God's Word. We know this because, in Acts 1:20, Peter quotes two passages from the Psalms that led him to conclude that this was God's will for the apostles.

Another example of a specific goal being set based on the knowledge of God's Word is in the book of Nehemiah. This is a great example of one of God's people standing on His promises and taking extraordinary action as a result. The book opens with some men visiting Nehemiah in Susa, where he was the cupbearer to the king. They came with news concerning Jerusalem, Nehemiah's hometown.

DISCOVER

Read Nehemiah 1:3. What was the reported condition of Jerusalem, and how did Nehemiah respond to this report?

_____

_____

So distraught was Nehemiah by this news that he spent several days weeping, mourning, fasting, and praying. What I love about Nehemiah is that he was a man of action. He wasn't content just to cry out to God about the condition of his beloved city. He was standing before God prepared to do something about it. After praising almighty God and then confessing on behalf of Israel, he recounted God's glorious promise to His people.

> *Remember the instruction you gave your servant Moses, saying, "If you are unfaithful, I will scatter you among the nations, but if you return to me and obey my commands, then even if your exiled people are at the farthest horizon, I will gather them from there and bring them to the place I have chosen as a dwelling for my Name."*
>
> —Nehemiah 1:8-9

Nehemiah was referring specifically to God's promise found in Deuteronomy 30:1-5, and he was resolved, based on his understanding of God's Word and His glorious promise, to take action consistent with God's plan. He was setting a very specific goal: to go back to Jerusalem and oversee the rebuilding of the wall. At the end of his prayer, Nehemiah, his new goal firmly in the forefront of his mind, asked God simply to give him success by granting him favor in the eyes of the king. God granted his request, and the king not only temporarily released Nehemiah from his service to pursue this project, he also ordered the provision of most of the materials that were needed to complete it. God's general promise to His people was the basis of a specific goal for Nehemiah, and it led to one of the most glorious accomplishments in Israel's history.

REFLECT

Have you ever set a goal based on a specific passage of Scripture? If so, explain.

_____

_____

On the opposite end of the spectrum, consider the Israelites as they arrived at the edge of the Promised Land. Moses recounted their disobedience in the first chapter of Deuteronomy, referring back to the time (detailed in Numbers 13) that Israel had sent spies to inspect the land. He had instructed them, _See, the_ LORD _your God has given you the land. Go up and take possession of it as the_ LORD, _the God of your fathers, told you. Do not be afraid; do not be discouraged_ (Deuteronomy 1:21). Hundreds of years earlier, God had promised this land on oath to Abraham's offspring. (See Deuteronomy 1:8, 29.)

The Israelites were well aware of God's promise, and now God had mercifully delivered them out of slavery in Egypt and brought them to the land that had been reserved for them. Unlike Nehemiah, who many years later would accept God's promises and plan accordingly, Israel quickly backed away from the objective.

DISCOVER

Read Deuteronomy 1:26. How did Moses characterize Israel's failure to obey God's instruction to go into the Promised Land?

_____

_____

_____

Taking possession of the land that God had promised them was a worthy goal for the Israelites, a goal that they would have set had they been inclined to heed God's Word. Their decision not to take action resulted in their wandering in the desert for another forty years.

David disregarded God's Word in his pursuit of an illicit affair with Bathsheba. Adultery evolved into murder when David tried to cover his tracks. This indiscretion cost David the life of his newborn son (2 Samuel 12:19), as well as public humiliation at the hands of his son, Absalom (2 Samuel 16:22). David repented and God graciously forgave him, but the temporal consequences continued, not only throughout David's lifetime, but for several generations as well.

These examples, Israel's failure to take possession of the land and David's moral failure with Bathsheba, were not the result of God's failure to provide clear instructions for His people. Rather, they resulted from God's people failing to set their priorities based on the instruction He provided.

REFLECT

Share an example of an instance in which you failed to take a particular action even though God's Word clearly instructed you to do so.

_____

_____

_____

_____

We've looked at God's people successfully setting goals based on knowing His Word, and folks who chose to ignore His Word in their pursuits. A final, and perhaps more relevant example for purposes of this discussion, involves the risk we take when we set our course *without the knowledge of God's Word.* This was the condition of God's people in the years leading up to the reign of King Josiah. During a succession of mostly wicked kings, God's people had increasingly ignored His Word. Israel's failure to study and submit to God's Word had led them into a life of blatant sin.

DISCOVER

Read 2 Kings 17:14-17. What were some of the practices engaged in by God's people as a result of their ignoring His Word?

_____

_____

_____

Is it unreasonable to suggest that this escalating pursuit of sin might have been avoided had God's people kept His Word constantly before them? Consider the response by Josiah when God's Word was finally brought to bear against the wickedness of His people. Let's try to picture the scene. The temple of God had fallen into great disrepair, and Josiah had assigned some men to undertake the necessary cleaning and renovations.

Have you ever had to clean out your basement, attic, or garage after many years of neglect? Stacks of boxes, old pieces of furniture, articles of clothing, piles of junk…things you've never needed or used, most of which you had forgotten existed. Yet in the process of sorting through the rubble, you stumble across a precious memory. Perhaps an old photo album, or a gift long ago received from a loved one. Much of what you've found will eventually be discarded, but this precious memory will be kept and enjoyed as if it were new. Such was the case with the temple as it was being prepared for renovations.

DISCOVER

Read 2 Kings 22:8. What was the "precious memory" that the High Priest discovered in the temple?

_____

_____

_____

_____

Imagine that — they found an old Bible in the church basement! Shaphan read aloud from God's Word a passage that described the curses that would befall God's people should they disobey His commands and instructions. Josiah was devastated at first, but then was convicted to take immediate action. He called together all of the people and read God's Word aloud to them. King Josiah *renewed the covenant in the presence of the LORD — to follow the LORD and keep his commands, regulations and decrees* (2 Kings 23:3). He proceeded to destroy all visible signs of idolatry throughout the land, and to put an end to those practices that were detestable in God's sight.

Why such heartfelt conviction and swift action? Because God's Word has power: power to convict us of sin; power to lead us into the path of righteousness; power to change a heart of stone into a heart of flesh. Throughout Scripture we see examples of hearts being transformed by the proclamation of God's written Word.

DISCOVER

Read Hebrews 4:12. What can we learn from this passage about the power of God's Word?

_____

_____

_____

_____

_____

Proper planning is the responsibility of all of God's people. Setting appropriate goals, as Nehemiah did, leads us to proper planning. I would submit to you that such planning cannot effectively be accomplished apart from God's Word. Our Father in heaven has spoken, and He granted that those words would be preserved in writing for the benefit of His people. God has a plan for your life and mine. *"For I know the plans I have for you,"* God assured His people through the prophet Jeremiah, *"plans to prosper you and not to harm you, plans to give you hope and a future"* (Jeremiah 29:11).

If we can accept my definition of a goal as "one aspect of God's plan for my life," we must develop an ongoing knowledge of God's Word in order to set goals that are consistent with His revealed will. I suspect that most of us have made mistakes in our lives that could easily have been avoided if we'd had a more thorough knowledge of Scripture. Goal setting requires godly wisdom, and such wisdom is found in His Word.

DISCOVER

Read James 1:5. How does this passage encourage us to seek God's wisdom?

_____

_____

_____

2. PRAYER – The second step in discerning God's will is fervent, expectant prayer. As we search Scripture and begin to develop a sense of God's plan for us, we should be engaged constantly in prayer, asking for His wisdom and direction as we plot our course. God expects us to plan, and He graciously promises to direct our steps as we do so.

DISCOVER

Read Proverbs 16:9 and Psalm 32:8. What is God's involvement as we make plans and set goals?

_____

_____

_____

_____

I memorized Psalm 32:8 many years ago and it still makes my heart pound when I consider it. Although I can scarcely comprehend this wonderful truth, my loving Father has a plan for my life, and He promises to reveal that plan to me as I seek Him. He provides ongoing teaching and instruction, showing me the way I should go. As I walk along in pursuit of His plan, He further promises to provide His counsel and to watch over me as I move ahead. This promise alone is sufficient to continually drive me back to my Father for guidance and direction.

How can we appropriate God's direction through prayer? The first step is to have repented of our sins and trusted in Jesus Christ, and Him alone, as our Savior and Lord. When faith in Jesus is professed, a wonderful "transaction" occurs.

DISCOVER

Read Ephesians 1:13-14. What happened when you heard the Gospel and responded by believing in Christ?

_____

_____

_____

_____

At the very moment you believed in Jesus, God the Holy Spirit was given to you, indwelling you until the day of Christ's return. If you are a follower of Christ, the Holy Spirit is presently indwelling you, guiding and enabling your prayers. It is possible for you to come to know the will of God because His Spirit is now a part of you. Even when you don't know what to pray, the Holy Spirit, who knows perfectly the mind and will of the Father, intercedes for you: *And he who searches our hearts knows the mind of the Spirit, because the Spirit intercedes for the saints in accordance with God's will* (Romans 8:27).

It can be difficult to explain just how the Holy Spirit guides us in prayer. This is a bit of a mystery. My experience has been that, as I seek God's will regarding a particular matter, I start to develop an increasing sense of conviction, of His clear leading. This is never a purely emotional experience. Rather, it involves my mind (certainty) and my will (desire), as well as my emotions. God's leading very often is contrary to the course I had started to pursue, but He changes my heart in the process and leads me to desire the course in which He is leading me.

REFLECT

Share an experience in which you sensed the clear leading of the Holy Spirit as you made a major decision or set a particular goal.

_____

_____

_____

One of the truly exciting things about this process is that there is almost always a sense of certainty. When God has spoken to your heart, you will generally know that He has done so. Keep in mind that this is not the only step in the process of discerning God's will, and it shouldn't be used in isolation. Prayer itself, of course, is a constant and ongoing part of the Christian life. But this kind of directed prayer, in which we are seeking to discern God's will with regard to a particular matter or course of action, should always be pursued in conjunction with the other three steps. Why? Because we can't trust our hearts. Even though we are in Christ, we still carry around the baggage of our sinful flesh: *The heart is deceitful above all things and beyond cure. Who can understand it?* (Jeremiah 17:9).

REFLECT

Share an experience in which a Christian has tried to justify a sinful action by insisting that the Holy Spirit led them to take such action.

_____

_____

_____

_____

_____

_____

My flesh continues to wage war against the Holy Spirit. Suppose I want to buy a new car that is really more expensive than I can afford. It is relatively easy for my flesh to convince my heart that God is leading me to make the purchase. I need to be willing to question my own motivation, and applying all four steps in this process allows me to do so before making an unwise decision.

Spending time in God's Word will often keep me from pursuing things that are not God's best for me. Prayer begins to provide the specific direction I need as I seek His will in specific areas of my life. _The prayer of a righteous man is powerful and effective_ (James 5:16).

3. COUNSEL OF MATURE CHRISTIANS – This third step in the process of discerning God's will is crucial, and yet it is often the most difficult. Why is it so hard for many of us to ask for help? It took many years as a Christian for me to get to the point of being willing to ask for counsel before making major decisions. I'm not sure exactly why, but I think pride had a lot to do with it. It always seemed like asking for help required admitting I didn't have all the answers. I learned in time that the only person who ever actually believed I did have all the answers was me. I prayed long and hard that God would begin to break down my sinful pride, and as He answered that particular prayer, it became much easier to seek counsel from mature Christians.

REFLECT

Identify one or several mature Christians from whom you would welcome advice and counsel.

_____

_____

_____

_____

_____

You'll notice that I keep stressing that those from whom we seek counsel must be "mature" Christians. This is vital. A new or immature Christian may be well-meaning, and more than willing to give you advice, but doesn't yet have the grounding in God's Word to give you consistently sound biblical counsel. Friends are most likely to tell us what we want to hear. A new Christian is often likely to give worldly counsel – not because they don't believe the Bible, but because they don't yet know what the Bible says about the issue with which you are struggling.

REFLECT

What characteristics distinguish a mature Christian from one who is immature?

_____

_____

_____

_____

I still remember the first time someone asked for my counsel when I was a new Christian. We were in a Bible study together, which I ended up leading by default. This friend was struggling with an important biblical principle, and asked for my help in understanding it. I confidently gave him an answer, one that seemed immediately to satisfy his concern. Several years later, as I was studying God's Word, the correct answer to his question became very obvious. The only problem was that it wasn't the answer I had given. He and I had since lost touch, and for all I know my friend still believes the Bible teaches something that it doesn't. The problem wasn't my lack of love for my friend, or my unwillingness to help. My problem was a lack of spiritual maturity and a very limited understanding of God's Word.

DISCOVER

Read 1 Corinthians 3:1-3a. What kind of counsel might we expect to receive from Christians whose faith is immature?

_____

For this reason, when you are seeking to discern God's will in a particular matter, seek out solid, mature Christians and ask for their counsel. Over time, you will develop a small group of caring and trusted friends who will always be willing to provide biblical advice as needed. I am blessed to have a number of such men and women in my life, and I'm convinced that the Lord will bring such friends into your life as well.

Just recently I was trying to make a decision about a practical financial matter. Both of the choices before me were acceptable as far as God's Word was concerned. I had a personal bias toward one of the choices, but as I prayed I couldn't get comfortable with my preferred decision. I couldn't tell if God was, at my specific request, directing me, or if I was just not ready to make a decision.

I decided that I needed counsel from one of my mentors. He listened patiently as I explained the two choices and my current leaning. He asked a few excellent questions, and then quickly concluded that one course of action was far superior to the other. What was great was how obvious the answer was once he talked me through it. I thanked my friend, and I thanked God for him. Years ago I would have found it extremely difficult to call and ask for help. Now I count it as one of my greatest blessings.

DISCOVER

Read Proverbs 13:10. What is one characteristic of those who are wise?

_____

Life is full of decisions, both minor and major. If you are proactively seeking God's plan for your life, and you desire His specific direction when making important decisions, or setting particular goals, this step is of vital importance. Please don't allow pride to keep you from availing yourself of the godly wisdom and counsel of Christians who are more mature than yourself. Your life will be enriched beyond measure.

DISCOVER

Write out Proverbs 13:10.

_____

_____

_____

_____

4. CIRCUMSTANCES – I'm almost reluctant to include this as part of the process, but God does use, and work through, our circumstances to give us His direction. My reluctance is based on the fact that many Christians make this their first priority in making a decision, and often never get around to the other three. One example might be a person who is struggling with debt due to a lack of spending discipline. Money is tight, as has been the case for many years. They need a break, a vacation…something to provide relief from the daily financial tension. They commit the matter to prayer, asking God to provide the means of relief. Suddenly, the mailman arrives with an application for a preapproved credit card with a $2,000 limit. Hallelujah! The desired vacation has now become a reality. God has answered – or so it seems.

This might seem a bit far-fetched, but you would be surprised at how many Christians have taken a preapproved credit card as God's answer to their specific prayers. That is what can happen when the process of discerning God's will begins and ends with your circumstances.

REFLECT

Share an experience in which you, or someone you know, relied purely on circumstances in taking an action that violated godly wisdom.

_____

_____

_____

_____

_____

Before discussing how we might appropriately use our circumstances as part of the process, let me provide a word of caution that is particularly applicable to making financial decisions. I'll preface this warning by noting that God's solution to our financial challenges is not always, or even usually, to provide access to more money. More often than not, financial challenges are the result of our poor stewardship, not a lack of sufficient income. We discussed earlier that the amount with which we are entrusted seems to be directly tied to our ability to properly manage those resources. Jesus makes clear in the parable of the talents that when we are unfaithful in our use of God's money, we risk having it taken away.

Like a loving parent who limits the amount of candy given to a child, despite the child's earnest pleading for more, our caring Father knows what is best for us, and He will act in accordance with His loving nature. If our financial challenges have arisen as a result of our neglecting God's instructions concerning the use of His resources, it is highly unlikely that He would answer our prayers by giving us more money.

Satan, on the other hand, is all too willing to bring additional "resources" to bear on our difficult circumstances, and that is the word of caution I want to share. Let's briefly review Luke chapter four, which describes the time that Jesus was led into the wilderness to be tempted by Satan. Three attempts were made to entice Jesus to sin, the second of which was the offer of wealth and power. How could Satan make such an offer?

DISCOVER

Write out Luke 4:6 and circle the words that indicate Satan had been given authority over the money and wealth with which he tempted Jesus.

_____

_____

_____

_____

_____

If you find yourself experiencing financial challenges and you are earnestly seeking God's direction in prayer, do not automatically assume that an offer of additional resources is necessarily God's answer to your prayers. Satan desires to draw you to himself, to lead you away from God's Word and into sin. That is why it can be dangerous to rely only on our circumstances in attempting to discern God's specific will for us. Satan will generally appeal to the flesh, and the flesh is usually an easy target.

DISCOVER

Read Genesis 3:6. What three things about the forbidden fruit led Eve to give into the temptation to disobey God?

1. _____

2. _____

3. _____

With those words of caution in mind, let's explore the ways in which our circumstances can be used to help us determine God's plan for our lives. The first way is that we use our circumstances to confirm or deny the direction we've received in the first three steps. When God is moving us in a particular direction, He will orchestrate our circumstances to fulfill His plan. If we have searched and understood God's Word, have spent time in prayer, and have sought the counsel of mature Christians to help us discern God's will in making a major decision, we can then look to our circumstances to confirm that decision.

In the Bible, Nehemiah serves as a great example of how God uses circumstances to confirm how He is leading through His Word and prayer. Regardless of how burdened Nehemiah was for the condition of Jerusalem and how convicted he was of God's promise to bring His people back to the city, his circumstances argued strongly against his being personally involved in such a pursuit. But once God had spoken clearly to his heart, Nehemiah's circumstances were quickly rearranged by God in order to confirm His plan and direction. It was extraordinary indeed for the king to release Nehemiah from his service in order to undertake this project, let alone to provide most of the materials needed for the repairs.

There are a number of other examples in Scripture of God's orchestrating the circumstances of His people in order to confirm the direction in which He is leading them. When making His covenant with Abraham (then called Abram), God promised to make him into a great nation, through whom all the nations of the world would be blessed, and whose offspring would be given possession of the Promised Land. There was just one problem. Abraham had no children; his wife had been unable to conceive and was now well beyond her child-bearing years. And the Promised Land was inhabited by the Canaanites, who had given no indication that they intended to give up their land. In time, however, God rearranged these circumstances in order to bring to pass those things He had promised.

Consider also the circumstances of two other heroes of the faith: King David and the apostle Paul. When the prophet Samuel anointed David as the one whom God had chosen to be king over Israel, David was but a young boy tending sheep and King Saul was already seated on the throne. When the risen Christ chose Paul (then Saul of Tarsus) as the one to preach the Gospel to the Gentiles, not only was he not even a believer in Christ, he was occupying his time with persecuting those who were. In both of these cases, as with Abraham many years earlier, God first provided the calling on His servant's life, and then He dramatically changed the circumstances to confirm His plan and lead them in the path He had chosen.

Have you ever had an experience in which God led you to a particular action and then changed your circumstances in order to accomplish His purpose for you? If so, explain.

_____

_____

_____

As we go through life making our various plans and decisions, let us be cautious about interpreting changing circumstances as God's primary means of revealing His will. Circumstances alone are not an accurate guide, especially when interpreted by a heart that is _desperately wicked_ (Jeremiah 17:9 KJV). However, once we have sought God's clear leading by studying His Word and through consistent, expectant prayer, and as that direction is affirmed through the counsel of mature Christians, pay close attention at that point to your circumstances. If God is truly leading in that particular direction, He will begin to rearrange your circumstances in order to confirm His calling and allow for its implementation.

DISCOVER

Read 1 Samuel 1:5-6,10-11,19-20. Once God had moved in Hannah's heart, how did He change her circumstances in order to fulfill His plan for her life?

_____

_____

_____

A Real-Life Example

The best personal example I can give to demonstrate the application of these four steps in discerning God's will involves a career change I made in 1994. I had been a stockbroker for ten years and, as I spent considerable time in God's Word studying biblical financial principles, I started to develop a sense of God's calling me to leave the brokerage industry. There were two significant obstacles, however. First, I had a contract with my current employer that I was sure restricted my ability to go elsewhere. Second, I had no skill or experience that would allow me to change jobs and continue earning the same level of income that I was currently earning and that I was sure I needed to continue providing for my family.

These obstacles were made even more challenging by the fact that, like Abraham, I had no idea where I was supposed to go. If the only criteria used to determine God's will was my circumstances, there was no need for further discussion. I had no choice but to stay put. Still, the conviction came with increasing intensity as I continued searching the Scriptures, seeking to understand God's plan for my life. I then committed the matter to constant prayer, and later began to seek out mature Christians to give me counsel on this important matter.

REFLECT

Have you ever experienced an increasing sense of conviction that God was leading you somewhere, but you had no idea where or why? If so, please explain.

_____

_____

_____

By the time I had implemented the first three steps in the process of discerning God's plan for my career, I was able to identify eight circumstantial obstacles that argued against taking the action I sensed God was leading me to take. Once again, if I had chosen to rely exclusively, or even primarily, on my circumstances, no further action would have been taken. By God's grace, however, the first three steps were leading me so clearly in the same direction that the obstacles got very little attention until toward the end of the process. I still remember the day of surrender, the point at which I committed to the Lord that I would leave my job and go wherever He would send me.

Suddenly, my circumstances began to change at a dizzying pace. One by one the seemingly insurmountable obstacles began to disappear. First, my wife and I prayerfully concluded that we had been living an overextended lifestyle and that we needed to significantly downsize in order to be faithful stewards of God's resources.

As a result of this downsizing, we would no longer need the same level of income I had been earning, which I was sure would be unavailable if I changed careers. Next, I came to learn of a firm that specialized in providing financial counsel from a biblical perspective. I knew immediately where God was sending me. This firm decided to open an office in the northeast, and they offered me a job in the new office so I wouldn't have to move my family out of state. Then my present employer willingly released me from my contract in exchange for my simply giving back my stock in the company. Ronald Blue & Company became the "Promised Land" for the Wise family.

Like a jigsaw puzzle being assembled in fast motion, God confirmed His plan for me by arranging my circumstances in such a way as to be unmistakably His work. I remember fondly a particular time of prayer in which I had written out the eight obstacles to making this career change. I laid the piece of paper in front of me and offered these circumstances up to my Father, noting their seeming impossibility and yet excited by the certainty that this was where He was leading. My wife and I watched in amazement as our Father cleared the way.

Summary

Spend time in God's Word learning the principles He has laid out for the proper management of His resources. Pray for clear direction as to what specific financial goals you should be pursuing. As you begin to formulate plans for the goals that God is laying on your heart, seek counsel from mature Christians, not only regarding the appropriateness of the goals themselves, but also asking for guidance in how best to implement your plans. Bring all of these things continually before the Lord, asking and trusting that He will direct your steps.

The Bible contains numerous examples of God's doing extraordinary things through very ordinary people. It is my prayer that you will trust Him to do such things in your life as well. *"I tell you the truth,"* Jesus said in John 14:12, *"anyone who has faith in me will do what I have been doing. He will do even greater things than these, because I am going to the Father."*

STUDY QUESTIONS

1. What has been your experience with trying to discern God's will for the specific decisions in your life?

_____

_____

_____

2. What are the four steps involved in discerning God's will (in order of priority)?

_____

_____

_____

3. How can a thorough knowledge of God's Word protect us from pursuing objectives that are unwise or unhealthy?

_____

_____

_____

4. What is the danger in relying exclusively on our circumstances in trying to discern God's will?

_____

_____

_____

5. In the past, how have you responded to Christians who seemed confident that they knew God's will for their lives?

_____

_____

_____

6. Will the information presented in this chapter help you in trying to discern God's will when you are faced with important decisions? Why or why not?

_____

_____

_____

Sample Financial Goals

GIVING

To increase my/our giving to _____% of gross income.

To provide monthly support to _____ as they serve in the Lord's work.

SAVING

To establish an emergency savings fund equal to three month's living expenses.

To add at least $_____ to my/our savings account each month.

To increase my/our monthly 401K plan contributions to $_____.

EDUCATION

To provide for my/our children to attend private school.

To provide for _____% of my/our children's/grandchildren's college expenses.

DEBT

To pay off all consumer debt within _____ months/years.

To pay off car loan(s) within _____ months/years.

To eliminate all credit-card use other than that which can be repaid within thirty days.

LIFESTYLE

To save $_____ in cash to pay for my/our next car.

To take a vacation to _____.

RETIREMENT

To have a retirement income of $_____ per month/year.

To purchase a retirement home in _____.

To be able to budget $_____ per month/year for travel in retirement.

MINISTRY

To go on at least one short-term missions trip each year.

To commit one week each year to serve the poor and needy.

- 8 -
SAVING
PART 1

"In the house of the wise are stores of choice food and oil..."

—King Solomon, Proverbs 21:20a

"...but a foolish man devours all he has."

—King Solomon, Proverbs 21:20b

Consider the circumstances of two retirees. Both were diligent workers in the same manufacturing facility, faithfully providing for their families during the forty-plus years of their employment. They lived in the same working class neighborhood and appeared to have virtually identical lifestyles. Both had a strong work ethic, rarely taking sick days and willing to work overtime when needed in order to make ends meet. Each family consistently gave tithes and offerings as the Lord continued to provide for all of their needs. Last year, at age sixty-five, both men retired with a modest pension and social security as the primary sources of income. Two families with strikingly similar circumstances now face dramatically different outcomes.

The first family, whom we'll call the Smiths, though living a relatively modest lifestyle, never gave much thought to budgeting or saving. They certainly lived within their means and their debt was generally limited to a mortgage and car loan. But they did have a tendency to spend what they earned. To their credit, they paid cash for almost everything. They took nice vacations but Mr. Smith would work weeks of overtime in order to set aside the money that was needed. They would purchase a new car every five years or so, but would not make the purchase until Mr. Smith had been given a raise that would ensure his ability to handle the larger car payment. Credit cards were rarely used except for convenience, and were almost always paid off immediately.

Since their modest lifestyle consumed all of their net income, their savings account never accumulated much above $1,000 or so. When major expenses were incurred, such as college tuition or home renovations, they were able to refinance their mortgage in order to use some of the equity that had built up rather than rely on student loans or credit cards. Finally, at retirement, the Smiths' finances were very much as they had been before: normal living expenses, mortgage and car payments, and just enough income to make ends meet. Their last mortgage refinancing, done three years ago to free some funds to update the kitchen and to take advantage of lower interest rates, still left them with an affordable payment. There were twenty-seven years left on the new mortgage. Similarly, the car was purchased several months prior to retirement, so there were four years left on the auto loan. Their living expenses total $2,000 per month and were covered by his social security ($1,000/month), her social security ($500/month), and his pension ($700/month).

They had always wanted to be able to travel in retirement, especially with the grandkids spread across several neighboring states, but there was no excess cash flow for anything beyond the basic necessities. This was not the retirement they envisioned. When the hot-water heater broke down and the decades-old air conditioner finally died, Mr. Smith began to contemplate taking a part-time job at the local hardware store in order to be able to generate the cash needed to cover these major repairs.

The Burkes, on the other hand, tended to look closely at their expenses every few months because they were committed to saving some amount for future needs. They would start years in advance setting aside a modest sum each month for such things as car replacement, home repairs, and college tuition. Ten years before their projected date of retirement, when the last of the kids was through college, they started adding $125 per month to the mortgage payment in order to pay it off prior to retirement. One of their fondest memories from the previous year was the celebration dinner they enjoyed after the final mortgage payment was made. For the first time in their life, they owned their home free and clear.

The company for whom Mr. Burke worked didn't offer a 401K plan until very late in his career. Although they did have a pension plan, Mr. Burke was never sure that it would be sufficient to meet their needs in retirement. As a result, way back when the kids were still small, the Burkes were diligent to set aside a small monthly amount in savings. At first they could only afford $25 per month. Over the years they increased this amount as they were able, and they had been saving $200 each month since age forty-five. This money had for years been automatically debited from the checking account and invested in a balanced mutual fund. Of course, when it came time to replace the cars they were unable to spend as much as they would have liked, choosing to buy newer used cars rather than brand new, but they felt like the sacrifice was worth it in order to be prepared for retirement. There were times, particularly during the college years, when the Burkes' vacations were limited to visiting relatives. They loved going to the beach for a week when they were able, and many family memories had been built there, but they were willing to occasionally forego the ideal vacation when money was tight rather than jeopardize their long-term plan.

Since their retirement last year the Burkes have been surprised by how well things are going financially. They didn't really know what to expect, and they had seen a number of friends, like the Smiths, retire and then struggle financially. As they prepare for a long-awaited cruise to celebrate their fortieth anniversary, they are rejoicing in God's faithfulness and provision in their retirement. Even with their frequent travel and having increased their charitable giving during the past year, the Burkes are still finding themselves able to save several hundred dollars each month. Why is their situation so different from the Smiths'?

To begin with, the Burkes have no mortgage payment. Their regular payment of $850 per month had been increased to $975 per month for the final ten years as they accelerated repayment in order to retire debt free. Since the mortgage is paid off, that amount is now excess cash flow. Also, the money they have faithfully saved each month has accumulated to nearly $300,000. They've decided to withdraw around 4 percent each year as supplemental retirement income, leaving the rest of the annual earnings to continue growing and compounding. Although their social security and pension income are virtually identical to that of the Smiths', they receive $1,000 more each month from investment income while their budget is $1,300 per month less as a result of retiring without a mortgage or car payment. In accordance with their long-term objective, the Burkes, while not considered wealthy by today's standards, have achieved financial independence in retirement.

If you had analyzed these two families over the years of their employment, you would have seen very little difference. Perhaps you would have noticed that the Smiths always had newer cars and took nicer vacations, but even those differences didn't seem very dramatic. Two families with years of very similar financial circumstances will spend their retirement years at entirely different economic levels. Why? It is the result of the Burkes' budgeting discipline over many years, combined with a commitment to saving some amount, no matter how small, rather than allowing themselves to consume every after-tax dollar that they earned.

REFLECT

Describe briefly your personal experience with creating, and adhering to, a monthly savings plan.

_____

_____

_____

_____

_____

Hindrances to Saving

During the last three or four decades the American mindset has shifted from encouraging disciplined saving to enjoying reckless spending. The priority is "me," and the time horizon is "now." Our marketing-oriented, consumer-driven culture has elevated instant gratification to the level of an eleventh commandment: "Thou shalt have whatsoever thou shalt want, whenever thou shalt want it" (my apologies to King James!). I suspect that the flesh has always struggled with an insatiable appetite for material things, but it might only be in recent decades that we've convinced ourselves that we actually deserve to have everything we want.

DISCOVER

Write out Proverbs 21:20.

_____

_____

_____

_____

_____

Spending restraint is not only a thing of the past; it is ridiculed as an outdated and repressive mode of thinking. Radio and television ads, billboards, and endless retail catalogues assault our senses daily with the mantra, "Buy Now, Pay Later." As a result, we've been increasingly enticed to buy what we cannot afford and to live a lifestyle that is above our means. Rather than get a raise and then increase our lifestyle, we now increase our lifestyle in anticipation of the raise. Rather than receive a tax refund and then spend it, we now spend it months before receiving it.

What does all this have to do with saving? For most folks, this new mindset has eliminated the practice of saving and replaced it with an emphasis on enjoying a higher standard of living. Whereas the Bible counsels us to plan for the future and live for others, our culture has conditioned us to live for today and care only for ourselves. We fail to save, not because we can't afford to, but because we would rather spend the money now. The availability of consumer credit, which will be discussed in a later chapter, has exacerbated this tendency by allowing us to live increasingly above our means. The portion of our monthly income that might otherwise be available for saving is needed to service the consumer debt we've accumulated.

REFLECT

How has advertising and our current culture impacted your spending habits?

_____

_____

_____

_____

We discussed in the last chapter the importance of planning by setting specific financial goals. These goals help us to cultivate a longer-term perspective and lead us to make spending decisions today that will help achieve our goals tomorrow. In the absence of such planning, there is no reason to save because there is nothing for which to save. Even if we instinctively know that saving is good, the daily temptation to improve our lifestyle overwhelms us. The process of goal setting helps us identify and focus on those things that we'll want or need in the future. This longer-term perspective is what will lead us to save a dollar rather than spend it.

There is another hindrance to saving that has become prominent, albeit unobtrusively so, during the past decade. It involves a common myth surrounding the projected amount of assets people need to accumulate in order to be able to retire. When I first entered the financial industry in 1985, the common assumption was that a person needed to accumulate a million dollars in order to achieve financial independence in retirement. In recent years that figure has inexplicably increased to between $2-3 million. I've talked to numerous people who were in anguish over having read an article that predicted a near-poverty-level existence for those who retire with less than this amount. I want to encourage you by dispelling this unreasonable assumption. I have counseled many families through the retirement process. One thing I know is that the majority of families that retire debt free will not require an unattainable nest egg in order to be comfortable.

REFLECT

What has been your impression of the amount of wealth you would need to accumulate in order to retire comfortably? Where did this impression come from?

_____

_____

_____

_____

_____

Consider our example of the Burkes at the beginning of this chapter. Their total retirement saving was $300,000, and this amount was accumulated by setting aside an amount that never exceeded $200 per month. Because they were debt free when they retired, their social security and pension alone were more than sufficient to meet all of their needs. The investment income was extra.

Think about a typical family's monthly budget. How much extra income would be available if such expenses as the mortgage payment, car payments, consumer debt payments, college loans, or other debt-reduction payments were eliminated? For most families, the remaining living expenses would probably not be very high. It is ludicrous to propose that the average family will need in excess of two million dollars in order to have a comfortable retirement. I've met many families who, despite having considerably less than that amount in assets, enjoy a more comfortable lifestyle in retirement than they did while they were working.

Reading such an article by some "financial expert" will discourage almost anyone from attempting to save. What's the point? If the absolute most I can scrape together is $100 per month for savings, and I'm in my mid-forties and only have twenty years left to save for retirement, I'm completely defeated before I begin if the accumulation goal is two million dollars. I might as well spend that $100 per month now and try to enjoy it because I'll never be able to retire anyway. This sense of hopelessness, fueled by so many writings that paint an inaccurate picture of retirement needs, has led many people to avoid any attempt at starting a regular savings program.

REFLECT

Give an example of a time when you became discouraged about your own prospects for retirement, either from the contents of a financial article or the opinion of a supposed financial expert.

_____

_____

_____

A third hindrance to saving money is simply failing to understand the biblical teaching on this subject. Just as many Christians will have no conviction regarding tithing until they are exposed to the biblical perspective, we'll also fail to understand the importance of saving unless we seek God's instruction. People are generally surprised to learn that savings and investment are even addressed in the Scriptures.

As with all things in life, our perspective and instruction should be derived from God's Word. We need to commit the time that is needed to discern God's teaching on this important topic.

An Example of Saving

One of the classic examples of saving in the Bible is in Genesis 41. Joseph was summoned from prison by Pharaoh in order to interpret two troubling dreams. Through these dreams God revealed that Egypt would experience seven years of abundance followed by seven years of famine:

> *"It is just as I said to Pharaoh: God has shown Pharaoh what he is about to do. Seven years of great abundance are coming throughout the land of Egypt, but seven years of famine will follow them. Then all the abundance in Egypt will be forgotten, and the famine will ravage the land. The abundance in the land will not be remembered, because the famine that follows it will be so severe."*
>
> —Genesis 41:28-31

DISCOVER

What important principle concerning our need to save can we learn from the above passage?

_____

_____

_____

Trouble was coming and God was gracious to give Pharaoh some advance notice. It is interesting that, now as then, difficult times tend to come on the heels of prosperous times. Those who have suffered through a severe downturn in the stock market know this feeling all too well. When the difficult financial times come immediately after a time of great prosperity, there is usually no warning and little, if any, time to prepare for the sudden downturn. That is why so many families can be devastated financially by the loss of a job or a major home repair. We are usually not prepared for such an event. If we are able to survive at all, it is usually by borrowing money rather than using funds saved during the good times. But there is a better solution. Consider the wisdom and practicality of Joseph's recommendation to Pharaoh:

> *"And now let Pharaoh look for a discerning and wise man and put him in charge of the land of Egypt. Let Pharaoh appoint commissioners over the land to take a fifth of the harvest of Egypt during the seven years of abundance. They should collect all the food of these good years that are coming and store up the grain under the authority of Pharaoh, to be kept in the cities for food. This food should be held in reserve for the country, to be used during the seven years of famine that will come upon Egypt, so that the country may not be ruined by the famine."*
>
> —Genesis 41:33-36

DISCOVER

How might Joseph's advice to Pharaoh in this passage be applied to our financial lives today?

_____

_____

_____

The focal point of Joseph's counsel was that it is wise to save during times of prosperity in order to be prepared for the difficult times that will inevitably come. In this case, the Egyptian officials were instructed to set aside 20 percent of all of the crops. For those of us desiring to apply this principle to our own finances, this might seem like an unreasonably high amount. It is interesting to note, however, that they weren't just storing up food for their own needs, but also to be in a position to help others.

> *When the famine had spread over the whole country, Joseph opened the storehouses and sold grain to the Egyptians, for the famine was severe throughout Egypt. **And all the countries came to Egypt to buy grain from Joseph,** because the famine was severe in all the world.*
>
> —Genesis 41:56-57, emphasis mine

We've seen in a previous chapter that one of the reasons God provides us with an income is so that we'll have something to share with those in need. Once we've determined an appropriate amount to save in order to meet our mid- and long-range financial goals, it is also prudent to save a little extra so that we're in a position to help those less fortunate through difficult economic times.

DISCOVER

Read Ephesians 4:28. How might the principle taught in this passage impact the percentage of our monthly income that we spend on our own lifestyle?

_____

_____

_____

_____

One recent example of Christians failing to heed this biblical advice occurred during the panic leading up to Y2K. Buying everything from weapons to freeze-dried food, from bomb shelters to real estate in the mountains, many who name the name of Christ dishonored Him by stressing self-preservation over ministry opportunity. Obviously, the disaster that was feared by many never materialized, but that isn't the point. If we were truly concerned about unrest in the cities, expecting that a shortage of food and drinking water would lead desperate families to loot their neighbors, why not spend God's money on extra food for those in need rather than weapons to protect what food we have? This was a sad time in church history, and our Christian witness was damaged as a result. Let us learn from Joseph's example and save a little extra in order to be in a position to help others should disaster strike.

DISCOVER

Read Proverbs 6:6-8. How does this passage reinforce the wisdom of saving?

_____

_____

_____

_____

Now that we have a basic understanding of how diligent saving can be a means of God's protection, and we've discussed several of the hindrances to saving, we'll turn our attention to the development of a consistent savings program. The next chapter will lead us in this process, as well as help us to develop some realistic expectations regarding the results of implementing such a plan.

STUDY QUESTIONS

1. What are three hindrances to a consistent savings program?

_____

_____

_____

2. Some financial writers have insisted that the average American will need to retire with $2-3 million in assets in order to live comfortably. How might such statements discourage us from attempting to develop a regular savings program?

_____

_____

_____

3. What general savings principle can we learn from Joseph's advice to Pharaoh in Genesis 41?

_____

_____

_____

4. How can Christians who exercise savings discipline be a blessing to others during difficult financial times?

_____

_____

_____

5. How did the response of many Christians to Y2K violate biblical principles regarding saving and giving?

_____

_____

_____

-9-
SAVING
PART 2

"Your gold and silver are corroded. Their corrosion will testify against you and eat your flesh like fire. You have hoarded wealth in the last days."
—James, the brother of Jesus, James 5:3

"He who gathers money little by little makes it grow."
—King Solomon, Proverbs 13:11b

An important biblical principle was developed in the last chapter as we looked at the wisdom of Joseph when he advised Pharaoh to store up excess resources during abundant times in order to be prepared for the famine that would eventually come. This action was blessed by God, and a remnant of His people who would otherwise have faced certain extinction were sustained by the food under Joseph's control in Egypt.

"Jim," you might be inclined to argue, "that was then and this is now. I like biblical history as much as anyone, but Pharaoh has been dead for a long time, and there is no famine in our land. Give me something practical, some motivation to start saving that makes sense in my life today." Fair enough. Let's take a look at some of the reasons that saving makes sense today, regardless of your income or economic level.

Reasons to Save

Following are several aspects of modern-day finances that make it prudent to develop a consistent savings program. Some of these factors have always existed, but some have only surfaced as concerns in recent years.

1. FINANCIAL EMERGENCIES – The most basic motivation to save a portion of our monthly income is the certainty of unexpected expenses. If you own a car or a home, there will come a time when something will break. If you depend on your car to get back and forth to work, a major car repair could certainly be classified as a financial emergency. Having an emergency reserve allows us to be prepared for such an expense so that it can be dealt with immediately. The same is true for uninsured medical expenses, home appliance repairs, and the sudden discovery of termite activity in your basement. When we heed God's advice and keep an emergency reserve to enable us to deal with these normal but unexpected expenses, we recognize God's provision for our daily needs. If we choose to ignore God's instruction by spending every dollar that we earn, these emergencies will inevitably be dealt with by increasing our debt load.

REFLECT

Share an experience in which a financial emergency arose and you were forced to use a credit card to pay for it due to a lack of savings.

_____

_____

_____

_____

2. PROSPECTS FOR RETIREMENT – I read a statistic several years ago that indicated approximately 80 percent of Americans retire with an income of less than $10,000 per year. I would imagine that the numbers have changed a bit since then to adjust for inflation, but the underlying problem most likely remains. Most people fail to prepare for retirement. In fact, my experience has been that the majority of folks don't even begin to think about retirement until several years before they plan to stop working. This seems logical enough. Prior to that time we are concerned with the necessary increases in lifestyle that accompany a growing family, things like getting the kids through college and paying for weddings. The next thing we know, the kids are gone, the nest is empty, and we have less than ten years to save for retirement. There are still a few employers around that have extraordinarily generous retirement plans, but most of us are on our own.

3. STRAIN ON SOCIAL SECURITY – I am not one who is concerned about the stability of social security, so I'm not hinting here that this part of your retirement income is in jeopardy. A relatively small increase in the FICA tax will extend the solvency of the system for many decades. However, since this system is currently funded on a cash basis, meaning that benefits being paid to retirees are being funded by current workers paying into the system, there will be increasing stress on the system as the baby boomers move through retirement.

When the social security system was created in the mid-1930s there were approximately thirty workers paying into the system for every one retiree drawing from it. Within two decades the ratio had declined to six workers per retiree, and by the mid-1990s there were less than three people working for every one drawing benefits. With the significant number of baby boomers moving into and through the retirement system, and with life expectancies continuing to increase, some structural changes will ultimately be needed to secure the system. Increasing the social security tax would seem the easiest and most obvious solution, and one that our leaders are generally willing to entertain, but that step alone will not provide adequate relief. There simply won't be enough workers paying into the system to support the large number of retirees.

I won't try to predict the eventual solution, but it is reasonable to assume one or all of the following: Benefits will be reduced; the taxation on benefits will increase; the annual cost-of-living adjustments on benefits will be reduced. Logic dictates that we should not expect the social security system alone to provide for all of our income needs in retirement.

REFLECT

What role do you expect social security to play in meeting your income needs in retirement?

_____

_____

_____

_____

4. CORPORATE RESTRUCTURING – It has become an increasingly popular strategy in corporate America to grow by merger and acquisition. When two large companies combine forces, there are generally two sets of management where only one might be needed. There might also be retail outlets or office facilities in the same town that can easily be combined into one. As a result, jobs are usually eliminated in the transition. Throw in the increased productivity that new technology provides, and job security becomes a thing of the past. We used to think in terms of securing a job with a solid employer and spending our career there. Such is no longer the case even if we want it to be. The fact is that most workers will change careers several times, and many of these changes are forced rather than voluntary.

I still remember the sadness I felt in counseling a local man who was about to be "downsized." His employer had been one of very few that for years was able to boast of having never laid off an employee. Now, as the result of a merger, they were planning to reduce the size of the combined work force. This man, who had an exemplary work record, was about to see his job eliminated. The severance package was modest at best and he could not afford to retire at age fifty-three. Where was he to go? Who would hire a man of his age and salary level when younger and less expensive candidates were available in abundance? I learned that day that job security doesn't exist in this generation.

REFLECT

How many different jobs have you had in your career? What impact has this had on your sense of financial security?

_____

_____

5. CHANGES IN RETIREMENT PLANS – It used to be that employers would favor defined-benefit pension plans, which are funded by the employer and provide retirees with a guaranteed income that is a percentage of their final salary. One of the most significant changes in retirement planning is the increasing use of defined-contribution plans such as 401K and 403B plans. These are primarily funded by employee (vs. employer) contributions, although some employers will provide matching contributions within certain limits. The bottom line is that even our employer's retirement plans are mostly dependent on our own ability to save. Even if you are among that rare breed of employee who ends up working for the same company for your entire career, if you are unable to make regular contributions to your employer's retirement plan, it is entirely possible that you will retire with no benefits at all.

REFLECT

Are you currently making contributions to a retirement program, either personal or employer sponsored? If not, what has hindered you from doing so?

_____

_____

_____

_____

My purpose is certainly not to shock or frighten you, but rather to encourage you that having a regular savings program is more important than ever. As the Burkes found out, it doesn't take an unreasonable amount of monthly savings, or a significant sacrifice to one's current lifestyle, to prepare for a comfortable and enjoyable retirement. It simply takes some planning and a little spending discipline. Once the proper habits have been created, very little effort is required to maintain a wise stewardship plan.

How to Save

The most important advice I can give on the process of saving is that it must be done as soon as we get paid, after our tithe but before our normal living expenses. The old adage "pay yourself first" applies. Most of us have tried the standard savings method of waiting until the end of the month to see how much money is left, planning to save the excess. We find out quickly that there is never any money left at the end of the month to be saved. For most of us, we're out of money several days too early and find ourselves counting the hours until our next paycheck. Suffice it to say that, in most cases, those of us who wait until the end of the month to save will not save anything at all.

Saving, like giving, is more important than continually increasing our lifestyle. If we are to be prudent in deciding what kind of lifestyle we can afford, it is imperative that we start by setting our giving level, paying our taxes, and setting aside our target savings amount. It is the money that is left that should be considered available for lifestyle, and even that amount is further reduced by debt service. If we take this approach to budgeting, we'll never have to worry about failing to save.

REFLECT

How much of your current income would you estimate is being spent on your lifestyle (as opposed to giving or savings)?

_____

_____

_____

_____

Once we've determined how much of our monthly income is to be saved, the next step is to remove it immediately from that "black hole" we call our checking account. If I had been asked to write the book of Proverbs, one of the first entries would have been, "As socks are sure to disappear from the dryer, so money will vanish from the checkbook." Even if you have an interest-bearing checking account and your paychecks are deposited directly into it, I would strongly suggest moving the savings immediately to another account. We are accustomed to spending what goes into the checking account, so any savings held there is usually at risk. The ideal solution is to open a separate savings or money market account and transfer the monthly savings amount into it.

If discipline has been a problem in the past, do not link the savings account to your checking account or your ATM card, or don't accept the checking option on the money market fund. Many folks won't have to go to this extreme, but it is advisable for those who have a tendency to spend whatever is available. Making it inconvenient to access the money will decrease the possibility of spending it prematurely.

REFLECT

How would you characterize your personal discipline when it comes to saving vs. spending? Why do you think that is so?

_____

_____

_____

One question that often arises as we begin to accumulate some funds in our savings account is, "Shouldn't I think about investing this money to get a better return?" My answer is that we shouldn't even think about investing until we have an adequate amount in savings to cover any emergencies that might arise, as well as any short-term purchases that we are planning. The interest rate on this money is not nearly as important as the liquidity, that is, your ability to get it when you need it.

The rule of thumb for an appropriate emergency reserve is between three and six months' living expenses. If your income is fairly stable and your job is secure, holding three months' living expenses in savings should be adequate. If your job is unstable, or if you are paid by commissions and have an income that is subject to wide fluctuations, the higher amount is warranted. For folks whose monthly budget is tight and who are unable to envision saving so large an amount without ignoring all other spending priorities, I would suggest the more modest initial objective of saving at least one month's living expenses.

REFLECT

Using the above rule of thumb, how much savings should you have as an emergency reserve?

_____

_____

Do you currently hold at least this amount in savings?

_____

_____

_____

If not, how many months of disciplined saving will be needed to accumulate this amount?

_____

_____

COMMIT

If your emergency savings fund is less than prudent, or if you haven't yet established this reserve, make a firm commitment today to accumulate the appropriate amount. Take this important issue to the Lord in prayer, asking Him to enable you to exercise the necessary discipline.

As you approach your target amount of savings for emergencies, the next step is to look around your home and try to determine what furniture or appliances might need to be replaced or repaired in the near future. Once you have a detailed list, determine how much needs to be saved each month for this purpose. For example, if you expect to replace your refrigerator in twelve months at a cost of $1,200, you'll need to set aside $100 each month for that purchase. If you are only able to save $50 each month, you'll want to change your time horizon to two years before making the purchase. The point is to try and have the cash saved before buying. This practice will protect you against accumulating an unwieldy amount of consumer debt.

REFLECT

Which items in your home will likely need to be repaired or replaced during the next few years and what is the expected cost?

_____

_____

_____

Next, consider other major purchases that will arise, such as car replacement, home improvements, or college tuition. The number and cost of each will determine how much additional monthly income needs to be saved. You might be saving for three different goals at the same time, such as a new refrigerator, auto replacement, and a home repair, but all of the savings will go into the same account.

Investing, as opposed to using a savings account or money market, comes into play when you are setting money aside for very long-term objectives. If you have money set aside for a child who starts college next fall, this is not investment money; it needs to remain safe and liquid. However, if you are starting now to save for college for your three-year-old, that money should most certainly be invested for long-term growth. Similarly, once sufficient funds have been accumulated for the shorter-term objectives, the money being set aside for retirement will also be invested for long-term growth. Asset allocation and investment strategies are topics that do not fall within the scope of this book, but there are many reputable advisors available to help you make appropriate investment decisions.

REFLECT

For what major long-term purchases or expenses should you be saving? What monthly amount will need to be saved to fund these objectives?

_____

_____

_____

_____

_____

_____

_____

_____

_____

_____

Result of Saving

The most obvious benefit of a regular savings program is that you'll always have funds available to cover the financial emergencies that will inevitably arise. As you have probably experienced, major appliance or auto repairs tend to be needed at the worst possible times. The car never breaks down just after we've received an annual bonus check or an unexpected tax refund. Such unbudgeted expenses more often occur when we have $5 in our checking account and a stack of bills that are slightly overdue. When we have no savings we tend to live in fear of the next financial emergency. With an adequate cash reserve, however, we feel secure in knowing that we have properly prepared for these expenses, and we can rejoice in God's provision when emergencies do arise.

There is one chart I would like to share with you because it might give hope to those starting later in life with making a commitment to a monthly savings program. The following chart depicts account balances at age sixty-five based on various savings amounts and interest rates. The purpose is to demonstrate how much you might expect to accumulate by retirement if you start your savings program today.

The Effects of Saving
and Compounding Interest
—Account Balances at Age 65—

SAVE $100 MONTHLY BEGINNING AT AGE:

INTEREST RATE	AGE 30	AGE 35	AGE 40	AGE 45	AGE 50	AGE 55
6%	$143,183	$100,954	$69,646	$46,435	$29,227	$16,470
8%	$230,918	$150,030	$95,737	$59,295	$34,835	$18,417
10%	$382,828	$227,933	$133,789	$76,570	$41,792	$20,655
12%	$649,527	$352,991	$189,764	$99,915	$50,458	$23,234

SAVE $200 MONTHLY BEGINNING AT AGE:

INTEREST RATE	AGE 30	AGE 35	AGE 40	AGE 45	AGE 50	AGE 55
6%	$286,367	$201,908	$139,292	$92,870	$58,455	$32,940
8%	$461,835	$300,059	$191,473	$118,589	$69,669	$36,833
10%	$765,655	$455,865	$267,578	$153,139	$83,585	$41,310
12%	$1,299,054	$705,983	$379,527	$199,830	$100,915	$46,468

SAVE $300 MONTHLY BEGINNING AT AGE:

INTEREST RATE	AGE 30	AGE 35	AGE 40	AGE 45	AGE 50	AGE 55
6%	$429,550	$302,861	$208,938	$139,305	$87,682	$49,410
8%	$692,753	$450,089	$287,210	$177,884	$104,504	$55,250
10%	$1,148,483	$683,798	$401,367	$229,709	$125,377	$61,966
12%	$1,948,581	$1,058,974	$569,291	$299,744	$151,373	$69,702

The interest rates selected are consistent with the long-term average returns on various types of mutual funds. (An experienced financial advisor can help you determine the appropriate investment strategy based on your age, objectives, and risk tolerance, as well as assisting with specific fund selection.) What I hope to demonstrate with these charts is that a considerable amount of money can be accumulated for retirement, even if we don't begin as early, or save as much, as we would have liked. Consider, for example, the second chart and the person who begins at age 45 investing $200 per month in a growth mutual fund with an average annual return of 12 percent. This person will retire with an account value of roughly $200,000. This might not sound like a lot, but a systematic plan withdrawing 6 percent per year thereafter will provide a supplemental retirement income of $1,000 per month. Most retirees would be blessed indeed to have an extra $1,000 per month in their income.

DISCOVER

Read Proverbs 13:11b. What important savings principle is noted in this passage?

_____

_____

_____

_____

_____

These charts obviously argue for starting early to save for retirement, and that is always the best advice. But we should be encouraged that, even for those of us getting started later in life, there is still hope. Never forget that the most important thing we can do to prepare for retirement is to pay off our debts. This dramatically reduces the amount of income that we will need to live comfortably, and it makes financial independence much more attainable, even if we are only able to save a modest amount each month.

Saving vs. Hoarding

A very common and legitimate question that often arises when discussing the topic of saving is, "How do I know when my saving becomes hoarding?" We understand from Scripture that saving is wise but hoarding is sinful. Distinguishing between the two is more complicated than simply selecting a dollar amount of savings that is not to be exceeded. Hoarding is a condition of the heart that includes selfishness, self-centeredness, and a lack of contentment. We've explored this problem in the chapter on materialism, but let's look more closely at a specific example of hoarding described in Luke's gospel.

DISCOVER

Read Luke 12:16-21. How did the "rich fool" demonstrate the sinful act of hoarding?

_____

_____

How did God respond?

_____

_____

This character in Jesus' parable saw all of his material wealth as belonging to him and being for his own enjoyment. Once his barns were full from his excess goods, he resolved to tear them down and build bigger barns so he could store even more stuff. So one indication that saving has become hoarding is when we see the thoughtless accumulation of material wealth that is well in excess of what one needs. Rather than begin to invest some of his wealth in kingdom work, the one who hoards keeps it all to himself, to his own detriment.

DISCOVER

Write out Ecclesiastes 5:13.

_____

_____

_____

Few people are more miserable than those who hoard. While pretending to be happy and content, they live in fear of losing what they've accumulated. They have few, if any, meaningful relationships because their lifelong focus has been on themselves: *People curse the man who hoards grain* (Proverbs 11:26).

Lack of generosity is a sure sign of hoarding. This can be done at any level of savings. When we cling too tightly to our money and possessions regardless of the needs around us, we are hoarding God's money. Hoarding differs from saving because it has no specific purpose or limit. It is accumulation for accumulation's sake. A closed heart leads to a tightly closed grip on the money one has saved. Such a heart becomes self-sufficient, forsaking the God who has provided the wealth and ignoring the kingdom work for which the wealth was intended.

REFLECT

How might the tendency to hoard impact a Christian's relationship with God?

_____

_____

_____

_____

One of the best ways I know to avoid hoarding is to have specific financial goals. All such goals, no matter how far into the future they might extend, can be quantified. There is a specific amount of savings that can be assigned to each goal. Even if the objective is financial independence in retirement, there is an amount of money based on the desired lifestyle that, once accumulated, will accomplish the goal.

In our example at the beginning of that previous chapter, the Burkes needed to save $300,000 in order to accomplish their retirement goals. Any significant accumulation above that amount could be safely considered excess. Your lifestyle may require more or less than the Burkes', but there is some amount that is ultimately sufficient. The same is true if you are saving for auto replacement, a new home, college tuition, or an inheritance for the kids. All financial goals can be broken down into some amount of necessary savings.

If we are regularly seeking the Lord's will for our lives and asking for His direction as to the financial goals that we should set, we'll always have some idea of how much savings will be needed to accomplish these goals. We will be much less likely to hoard God's resources because we'll know when we've accumulated more than we need. The faithful saver experiences joy both in the accumulation of God's resources for specific financial goals and in the giving away of excess resources. The one who hoards, on the other hand, knows no joy regardless of the amount accumulated. As you begin to experience success in saving the resources that are needed to fund your financial goals, pay close attention to the condition of your heart. If you feel your grip beginning to tighten around the resources God has provided, it is probably time to give some of it away. Be diligent to save as God has instructed, but beware of hoarding His resources in the process.

Saving Tips

We'll close with several biblical points to consider as we commit to a regular savings plan. If you've struggled in the past with saving, I want to encourage you to commit this matter to prayer. God is faithful, and His Spirit will enable obedience as we seek His help. Disciplined saving is not only enormously beneficial, but it is also a practice that is encouraged in the Scriptures. Here are a few savings tips from God's Word.

1. SAVING IS WISE. We all desire to exercise godly wisdom, both for our own benefit and as a matter of obedience to our loving Father. God has given us many financial principles to live by, and saving is one of them. Remember His counsel in Proverbs 21:20: *In the house of the wise are stores of choice food and oil, but a foolish man devours all he has.* Wisdom demands that we commit to a lifestyle that allows for regular and consistent saving.

2. SAVING IS PROFITABLE. Contrary to the get-rich-quick mentality that leads many to financial ruin, Proverbs 13:11 promises that *he who gathers money little by little makes it grow.* The key is consistency and discipline. Our savings will accumulate quickly if we are committed to adding to them each month. This practice will ensure the successful achievement of our financial goals.

3. SAVING IS OUR RESPONSIBILITY. In our effort to apply God's Word to our finances, it is important to understand that saving is not just a good idea, it is a requirement. We are taught in 1 Timothy 5:8 that *if anyone does not provide for his relatives, and especially for his immediate family, he has denied the faith and is worse than an unbeliever.* Part of providing for our family includes both having an emergency cash reserve and setting aside funds for future needs that we won't be able to cover out of our regular cash flow. God supplies the income and instruction, and we are responsible to use both to properly provide for our families.

4. SAVING OFFERS GOD'S PROTECTION. We've observed this principle at work in the account of Pharaoh and Joseph in Genesis 41. Egypt and the surrounding nations were able to survive a severe famine because of the saving that was done in the years leading up to the calamity. God's people would likely have become extinct were it not for Joseph's exercise of godly wisdom at this crucial time in history. Financial challenges are a normal part of life, and economic cycles include both the good and the bad. Let us learn from Joseph's example and prepare in advance for the financial challenges that will inevitably come our way. *A prudent man sees danger and takes refuge, but the simple keep going and suffer for it* (Proverbs 22:3).

Now that we are giving regularly to God's work, have established some specific financial goals, and have committed to a consistent savings program, we are ready to move on to the fourth step in the process of achieving financial freedom: budgeting.

STUDY QUESTIONS

1. What is the danger of failing to establish an emergency savings fund?

_____

_____

_____

2. How do we determine the proper amount that should be held in savings?

_____

_____

_____

3. Why is there much less job security in this generation than in prior generations?

_____

_____

_____

4. In addition to a consistent savings program, what is the most significant financial step we can take in preparing for retirement?

_____

_____

5. When does saving become hoarding?

_____

_____

6. How can failing to save violate the biblical command to provide for one's family?

_____

_____

_____

-10-
BUDGETING
PART 1

"Suppose one of you wants to build a tower. Will he not first sit down and estimate the cost to see if he has enough money to complete it?"
—Jesus, Luke 14:28

"The plans of the diligent lead to profit as surely as haste leads to poverty."
—King Solomon, Proverbs 17:16

Most folks experience an immediate sense of tension and anxiety at the very mention of the word *budget*. When I first began teaching on the subject of biblical stewardship, it was my expectation that the greatest resistance encountered would involve the topic of giving. Not so. By far the most unpopular issue in a financial discussion is budgeting. Since I had started budgeting early in life, and never found it particularly tedious, I was somewhat confused by the reaction I usually got when teaching on this subject. I've since discovered that most of the tension has to do with a misunderstanding of the purpose and process of budgeting. If you are among those whose list of priorities ranks budgeting just below having a root canal without anesthesia, take heart. You'll soon see how maintaining a monthly budget can create a sense of freedom that you might not be experiencing at present.

REFLECT
What has been your personal experience with using a budget?

_____

_____

_____

_____

The most common reaction to the thought of budgeting is that of feeling "restricted." We think of a budget as a rigid set of rules that leaves no room for discretionary spending of any kind. Perhaps this is because one characteristic of our sin nature is our reluctance to be told what to do. Even if we are the ones creating the rules for ourselves, we resist the idea of setting any spending restrictions on our monthly income. We want the freedom to do as we please. Interestingly, most folks acknowledge that their financial condition would be considerably improved if they planned their expenses. Still, the thought of exercising the spending discipline inherent in the budgeting process leads most of us to resist the idea, no matter how desperately we might need it. The starting point, then, is to deal with the natural sin that causes most of us to resist any exercise of spending discipline. This sin is usually at the root of our refusal to budget.

The Lack of Discipline

Most of us recognize the need we have for discipline, but our flesh works against us at every turn. This struggle goes all the way back to the Garden of Eden. God had created a beautiful world, and *it was good* (Genesis 1:25). Then He created Adam and Eve and blessed them by giving them dominion over all that He had created.

DISCOVER

Read Genesis 1:28-29. What can be said about God's material provision for Adam and Eve?

_____

_____

_____

Of all of the fruit-filled trees in the Garden, God made specific mention only of the two trees in the middle of the Garden: the tree of life and the tree of the knowledge of good and evil. Adam was instructed not to eat from the latter, upon penalty of death.

DISCOVER

Compare Genesis 2:9 with Genesis 3:6. What similarities do you see in the two descriptions?

_____

_____

Why do you think the forbidden fruit became more appealing to Eve than the other fruit?

_____

_____

There may be several possible answers to the preceding question, but I suspect that what made this particular fruit so appealing was the prohibition against eating it. Given the fact that all of the trees were equally appealing for their fruit, it would seem logical that the fruit they were allowed to eat should have been favored over that which would bring certain death. But Adam and Eve, persuaded by Satan that they would not die, and that if they ate they would _be like God_ (Genesis 3:5), gave in to the temptation and disobeyed their Creator. Given countless blessings and only one rule to follow, Adam and Eve chose disobedience. We deceive ourselves if we believe we would have chosen any differently. Rebellion against authority is deeply ingrained in our sinful flesh.

REFLECT

How does a young child usually react when told not to touch something? How would you explain this behavior?

_____

_____

_____

Imagine that you are standing in the produce aisle of the largest supermarket in your town. You stand gazing at the beautiful display of every kind of fruit and vegetable imaginable, all pleasing to the eye and good for food. The department manager tells you that it is all yours — free. Take whatever you want, and when you need more, come back and help yourself. But there's one exception. There is just one piece of fruit, halfway down the aisle on the right, between the bananas and the oranges, that is off limits. Take whatever else you want, but don't touch that particular piece of fruit. Think about it. Doesn't that one piece suddenly seem irresistible? For some reason, the very thought that we can't have it makes us want it all the more. One of the many evidences of our sinful nature is our always wanting what we cannot have. This is the lack of contentment discussed in an earlier chapter.

What does this have to do with budgeting? Two things. First, we have a natural resistance to being told what to do, and budgeting makes us feel like someone is standing over us, telling us what we may or may not buy with our own money. Second, many of us are naturally lacking in contentment, and we seek the temporary pleasure that derives from buying things that we can't afford. If we blithely proceed from month to month never looking at how our expenses compare to our income, we don't have to feel confronted by our overspending. Out of sight, out of mind. Credit cards (which will be discussed in a later chapter) allow us to accumulate things that we truly cannot afford. When we combine the lack of a budget with the indiscriminate use of credit cards, we are able to live for a long period of time above our actual means.

A written budget, on the other hand, is like a mirror that exposes every wrinkle and imperfection. If I keep a budget and spend $200 more than I earn this month, I am immediately confronted by my indiscretion. I can't ignore the problem because it is right there in front of me, in black and white. Since most of us don't like to feel bad or guilty, we default to poor stewardship by refusing to budget.

DISCOVER

Read Proverbs 21:5. Explain how this passage might relate to budgeting.

_____

_____

_____

Why Budget?

In a prior chapter we looked at the necessity of planning, and budgeting is an important part of the process. Planning requires thought and a long-term perspective, whereas a lack of planning requires no effort at all. Without planning our monthly expenses by creating a written budget, we are left to making a series of hasty decisions that are driven by our flesh. If I see something I want, I'm never confronted with whether or not I can afford it because I haven't set any spending limits. My income is irrelevant because my expenses are unknown. If I want it, I can buy it. If I don't have the money in my checking account, I can charge it. If I make the monthly payments on my charge card, I reason, it will eventually get paid off. This is the essence of hasty, or impulsive, decision-making, and God says that will surely lead to poverty.

DISCOVER

Read Proverbs 27:12. How can preparing a budget help to protect our finances?

_____

_____

_____

_____

_____

Our commitment to preparing a monthly budget will enable us to see potential spending problems in advance. As a result, we are able to "take refuge," or avoid making decisions that will later cause us to suffer. *Go to the ant, you sluggard; consider its ways and be wise! It has no commander, no overseer or ruler, yet it stores its provisions in summer and gathers its food at harvest* (Proverbs 6:6-8). Budgeting involves planning ahead, which allows time to prepare for those irregular expenses, such as Christmas or a vacation, that lead many into increased debt and financial hardship. Those who budget are far less likely to overspend, and much more likely to diligently plan and prepare for future expenses.

DISCOVER

Read Proverbs 21:20. What will likely result from failing to plan our expenses?

_____

_____

One who budgets is also more apt to have an emergency cash reserve and to leave some excess cash flow each month for unexpected expenses. Those who have chosen not to budget are much more prone to "devour" every dollar that comes in.

It is easy to discern from Scripture that budgeting is preferable to failing to plan. Why, then, is it so difficult to make this commitment? In addition to our disdain for being told what to do, as discussed previously, we also have a natural resistance to exercising discipline. We all have our weaknesses, be it chocolate, fast food, soft drinks, television, shopping, or a myriad of other things. Enjoyed in moderation, such things can be a blessing. When taken to excess, however, each can quickly become detrimental to our physical, spiritual, or financial health. This is why exercising discipline is so important, particularly in relation to spending God's money. The alternative is almost certain financial stress and anxiety.

DISCOVER

Read Proverbs 13:18. What will happen to those who ignore discipline?

_____

_____

_____

_____

_____

If you, like most folks, have found it almost impossible to exercise such discipline in your life, I have good news. One fruit of the Spirit is self-control (Galatians 5:23), so we can take comfort that whatever past struggle we might have faced in exercising personal discipline, the Holy Spirit is with us to strengthen and enable us. It goes without saying, however, that we need to seek self-control in order to obtain it. We don't lack discipline because we are incapable of it; we lack discipline because we are unwilling to exercise it. We must first understand that, not only is discipline godly, it is also good for us. When we understand the personal benefits of exercising spending discipline, we'll find that it isn't that difficult after all.

REFLECT

If you are not currently using a budget, what has hindered you from doing so? What has been the result?

_____

_____

_____

_____

Preparing to Budget

How do we come to understand the benefits of budgeting, that we might be constructively motivated to do it? We can start by seeking counsel from someone who is committed to the budgeting process. Find a mature Christian friend who has been implementing biblical principles in managing their finances, and ask them to share what the impact has been. Ask about the benefits of planning their spending and how God has blessed their obedience. I suspect that a few such conversations with faithful followers of our Lord will provide more than sufficient motivation to start planning your monthly spending.

The next step is accountability. Once we have understood that budgeting is an important part of the stewardship process, and that God's Word encourages both wise planning and spending discipline, it is a good idea to ask a trusted friend to hold you accountable for following through.

DISCOVER

Read Proverbs 27:17 and Ecclesiastes 4:9-10. What encouragement can we take from these passages with regard to accountability relationships?

God does not intend for us to live out our faith in isolation. Our sinful nature is a formidable foe, and we often need the help and encouragement of other like-minded friends when attempting to change. Internally, as noted previously, we are blessed to have the Holy Spirit, granting us His wisdom and guidance while empowering us to obedience. Externally, we are blessed when we have others walking with us. If I invite a close friend to hold me accountable for creating a monthly budget, I am more likely to follow through. If I struggle to implement it, my friend will lovingly "pick me up" and encourage me to move forward. It is true that we will often do something for a friend that we won't do for ourselves. That is why accountability partners are such a blessing.

List below several friends who are financially responsible and who might be willing to hold you accountable in the area of stewardship.

1. _____

2. _____

3. _____

Understanding Your Budget

Simply defined, a budget is a spending plan. The purpose of creating a budget is to plan our monthly expenditures, to determine *in advance* how much of our income we are comfortable allocating to each spending area. Each of us has some amount of money that God entrusts to us each month. Our job is to divide this income among the various needs and wants that we have.

Far from being restrictive, budgeting actually provides a sense of freedom. If I like to play golf, or to go out to dinner, the act of budgeting does not prevent such discretionary spending. Rather, a properly designed budget actually allows me to enjoy such spending *without guilt*. Why? Because I'm setting aside money specifically for this purpose, and only after first setting aside money for the nondiscretionary expenses that occur each month. Budgeting doesn't prohibit my playing golf each month. Rather, having a budget causes me to ask the question, "How much of this month's income am I comfortable allocating to golf?" The amount of golf I play, or the number of dinners out, is determined in concert with my other spending priorities.

There is nothing wrong with using part of our income for pleasure. The problem comes when we use a disproportionate amount of our income on discretionary spending while ignoring our other responsibilities. That is what happens when we fail to plan. The flesh being what it is, if I fail to budget I am likely to spend more on leisure than I can really afford, to the detriment of other spending areas that may be of greater importance. One example might be a family that is a couple months behind on their car payment but that continues to eat out once or twice each week.

The problem is not the practice of eating out, it is the frequency, as well as a failure to treat the car payment as the greater responsibility. Eating out is not a contractual obligation, but a car payment is. When we fail to honor our other financial obligations because we are spending an unreasonable amount on personal pleasure, that is when we are guilty of abusing the resources God has entrusted to us.

REFLECT

How can failing to plan monthly expenses lead to guilt over money spent on pleasure (i.e., wants vs. needs)?

_____

_____

_____

_____

On the other hand, once I've created a monthly budget and allocated the proper amount of income to the nondiscretionary areas (i.e., mortgage, car, insurance, food, utilities, etc.), then I am free to divide what remains among the discretionary expenses. The result is that, when I play golf or eat out, there is no guilt over spending that money because I do so as part of the overall spending plan. Once I have spent the amount allocated to that activity, I am finished for the month. No questions; no guilt. This leads to the common question about the specific expenses that are to be included in the budget. Some are clearly laid out in Scripture, whereas others require the exercise of godly wisdom in accordance with general biblical principles.

Budgeting Priorities

The first step in creating a budget is to examine the priorities that God has directly revealed in His Word. There are five general budget categories that are clearly mandated: giving, taxes, saving, living expenses, and debt repayment. I'll begin with the bad news: God doesn't give us specific amounts that are appropriate for each area. We have seen that tithing is a responsibility of all of God's people, but many people are led to give considerably more than a tithe. We learn in God's Word that saving is wise, but we are not instructed as to how much we should save, or when the obedient practice of saving becomes the unbiblical practice of hoarding. There are no specific amounts, only guidelines. The amount that God calls on you to give or save might be dramatically different from what He calls me to do. Both of us, however, are to be involved in giving and saving. Let's take a look at those budget categories that are clearly defined in the scriptures.

GIVING IS PART OF THE BUDGET. We have already addressed this area at length so I won't be redundant here. It is important to realize, however, that one of the reasons God gives us an income is to enable us to share with those in need.

DISCOVER

Read Ephesians 4:28. How is this teaching contrary to the way most of us think about the purpose of earning income?

_____

_____

_____

Most Christians understand the practice of using our earned income to provide for ourselves and our families, but we probably don't think of it as being for those in need as well. When you've been on the receiving end of such generosity, as I have been, this verse takes on considerably greater meaning. This is why it is important to budget in such a way as to allow for some excess. Then we are able to respond when we see someone in need.

Giving is an important part of the budget because we live in a fallen world and are surrounded by people in need. Offering to pray with and for such folks is fine, but that is not all that God requires of us.

DISCOVER

Read James 2:15-16. What is our implied responsibility when we encounter someone in need?

_____

_____

Even in America, one of the most prosperous nations in the world, such opportunities present themselves with increasing regularity. As you read the Gospels you will note that Jesus was continually meeting the physical needs of the people He encountered. He healed the sick, fed the multitudes, expelled demons, and gave sight to the blind. Jesus is our model of loving compassion. Many of those to whom Jesus ministered never did become His disciples, but that never stopped Him from caring for their physical needs. The same should be true of us.

REFLECT

To what extent has giving been a part of your monthly expenditures?

_____

_____

SAVING IS PART OF THE BUDGET. The previous chapter was devoted to this important area, so we've seen that part of our income is to be saved for future needs. If we spend every dollar that we bring home each month, we are never prepared for emergencies or unexpected expenses that will inevitably arise. Saving provides consistent evidence of God's provision that we would not otherwise enjoy. When the hot-water heater breaks down or the roof needs repair, if we have diligently set aside some funds each month, we can rejoice in God's provision for that unexpected expense.

DISCOVER

Take another look at Proverbs 21:20 and 22:3. What do these passages teach about the importance of saving?

_____

_____

_____

When we neglect our responsibility to prepare in this way, and we don't have the money to make the needed repairs, it is we who have failed, not God's Word. One of the primary ways in which God provides for our material needs is not only by giving us an income, but also through the financial principles He has given us in His Word to enable us to properly manage this income.

TAXES ARE PART OF THE BUDGET. Whether or not we agree with the government's use of our tax dollars, one thing is clear: God instructs us to pay them. It is certainly prudent to minimize our tax burden by taking advantage of the various deductions that are allowed under the tax code, but there is no question that God requires us to pay our taxes, whatever amount we legitimately owe.

DISCOVER

Read Romans 13:6-7 and Luke 20:25. What do these passages teach about paying our taxes?

_____

How does Jesus reinforce this principle in Matthew 17:24-27?

_____

_____

_____

DEBT REPAYMENT IS PART OF THE BUDGET. This is another area that will require two full chapters to fully explore, but the Bible is clear as to our responsibility where debt is concerned. If we borrow money, it must be repaid. Most loans are contractual obligations, but *all* loans are moral obligations.

DISCOVER

Read Psalm 37:21. What term is used to characterize someone who fails to repay a debt?

_____

_____

Timely repayment of our debts is an important part of our Christian witness, and many of us are failing the test. We borrow more than we can afford, and then we seek the sanctuary of the bankruptcy laws to have such debts extinguished. I might be in the minority on this issue, but my firm conviction based on God's Word is that filing bankruptcy does not eliminate our moral obligation to repay our debts.

DISCOVER

Read Romans 13:7-8. Write two phrases that address our responsibility to repay our personal debts.

1. _____

2. _____

There might well be a time when a creditor extends mercy by offering to cancel a debt that we are struggling to repay. Such an offer is just another example of God's infinite grace and mercy. In all other cases, however, we are obligated to repay any and all amounts that we have borrowed, regardless of how long it takes to do so. Debt repayment is an important part of our monthly budget, and it is one of the priorities.

LIVING EXPENSES ARE PART OF THE BUDGET. If ever there was an area of finance in which I've longed for additional biblical instruction, this is it. We constantly struggle with lifestyle decisions: new or used car; smaller or larger home; when to replace the furniture, etc. The problem many of us face is that, since we haven't ever used a written budget, we really don't know what kind of lifestyle we can reasonably afford. As a result, we look at monthly payment amounts rather than total cost and we often confuse needs and wants. By the time most of us get around to reading a book like this, we have already committed our entire after-tax income to our lifestyle. That makes it quite a challenge to begin tithing, saving, or accelerating debt repayment.

Although the Bible doesn't tell us how much to spend on our living expenses, it does give us some basic guidelines that are helpful. The first is that, if I have a family, I'm responsible to provide for their basic needs.

DISCOVER

Read 1 Timothy 5:8. What two statements does Paul make to describe a person who fails to provide for his or her family?

1. _____

2. _____

Whether we live alone or are responsible to care for a family, there are basic needs that must be met before money is committed to discretionary expenses. Failure to do so, especially with regard to our immediate family, is tantamount to denying our faith. It goes without saying that needs supersede wants, and when money is tight we must be willing to forego some of our wants in order to be faithful to this biblical admonition. When faced with a choice between a need (a nondiscretionary expense) and a want (a discretionary expense), the need is the greater priority.

I remember counseling a young couple that was struggling to make ends meet each month. As we reviewed their regular monthly expenses and worked to develop a budget, we discovered a significant amount each month being spent on the husband's favorite hobby. His wife was diligently clipping coupons and shopping for sales in the supermarkets, but she just didn't have enough money each month to provide the food that was needed for the family. The problem was not that she was overspending; on the contrary, she was extremely frugal and responsible with the grocery money that she was given. The problem was that the amount available for food was inadequate because her husband chose to make his personal hobby a priority over providing food for the family.

As you can imagine, there was tremendous tension, stress, and anxiety each month, with the wife frustrated that her food budget was unreasonably small and her husband frustrated with his wife's apparent inability to stay within the allotted amount. This is a surprisingly common occurrence among families that don't budget because the problem is never obvious until it is on paper. Prior to their creating a monthly budget, this couple had no idea what the specific problem was or how easy it was to solve. The husband wasn't purposely failing to provide for his family, but that is what was happening because there was no written budget. Happily, creating a monthly budget identified the problem and led to the solution.

Read 1 Thessalonians 4:11-12. What might eventually happen if we were to consistently live above our means?

_____

_____

_____

_____

If we set a lifestyle that is too high for our income, we will eventually be unable to pay our bills or repay our debts. This leads to dependence on others as we are then forced to ask friends or family to lend us money or we must turn to the church for financial assistance. To be sure, there are times when such assistance is legitimately needed, and God's people are always willing to respond in love. There are times, however, that the reason for the shortfall is purely the result of foolish spending.

When we spend God's money on our wants before meeting our family's needs, we dishonor God and undermine our Christian witness. Our daily life, at that point, fails to win the respect of others, especially those to whom we continually turn for help to bail us out of our consistent pattern of irresponsibility. The key to setting a good example and to avoiding dependence on others is to plan our spending in advance, making sure to cover all of the areas mandated by Scripture. Success in this area, for the vast majority of people, requires a monthly budget.

STUDY QUESTIONS

1. What area of sin is often responsible for the failure to plan our monthly expenses?

_____

_____

_____

2. What are some of the positive aspects of budgeting?

_____

_____

_____

3. For those struggling with planning or spending discipline, what step can be taken to provide accountability?

_____

_____

_____

4. What are the five general expense categories?

_____

_____

_____

_____

5. Has any of the information in this chapter changed or reinforced the way you think about budgeting?

_____

_____

_____

-11-
BUDGETING
PART 2

"I was young and now I am old, yet I have never seen the righteous forsaken or their children begging bread."

—King David, Psalm 37:25

"And my God will meet all of your needs according to His glorious riches in Christ Jesus."

—The Apostle Paul, Philippians 4:19

As we discussed in the previous chapter, budgeting our living expenses is challenging because God doesn't give us specific amounts or percentages for each area. The best way to make our lifestyle decisions, then, is to first consider the other spending priorities that God has defined for us. Doing so will make the decisions concerning lifestyle much easier. For example, let's assume that you've never given regularly to the Lord's work but you are now joyfully convicted that you should. Perhaps you set as your initial target giving 10 percent of your gross income. Assume further that you decide that it is prudent to save a like amount, and your tax withholding equals 20 percent of gross income. These three categories will require 40 percent of your total income, leaving 60 percent for lifestyle, including debt repayment. If you have some debt already, simply subtract that monthly payment amount from the 60 percent, and the rest is available for other living expenses, both discretionary and nondiscretionary.

This process simplifies decision-making considerably because we have a set amount to devote to our lifestyle and, as we budget that amount, we do so knowing that our other biblical priorities have already been met. The Bible doesn't tell us how big of a house to buy or how much to spend on a car, but using the other four spending categories as a guide will help us prudently determine how much we have available for such living expenses.

As we proceed to look at the specific details of preparing a monthly budget, please note that this chapter will deal mostly with actual living expenses as opposed to giving, saving, and taxes. These areas have been addressed in detail in previous chapters, so we'll assume that these amounts have already been committed prior to budgeting your actual living expenses.

APPLY

Approximately what percentage of your monthly income is currently being used for each of the following areas?

Giving: _____% Saving: _____% Taxes: _____% Debt: _____%

How much does that leave for your living expenses? _____%

Budgeting Process

Even if you have never attempted to create a monthly budget, it is not as difficult as it might seem. The starting point is to get a copy of a budget worksheet such as the one included at the end of this chapter. It is better to start with this as a guide rather than using a blank sheet of paper and trying to remember all of your expenses. You'll want to have your checkbook handy, as well as your copies of the bills from the past several months, if you save them. The objective is to complete the budget worksheet, starting with the nondiscretionary (or fixed) expenses, using your average actual spending figures for expenses that vary slightly from month to month. The fixed amounts are easy, such as your rent or mortgage, car payment, cable TV, and Internet service provider. Then move on to the fixed expenses that vary, such as gas and electric bills, food, and telephone service. By glancing back at recent bills, or reviewing your checkbook, you'll find it easy to budget an appropriate amount for each expense.

APPLY

To help you get started in the budgeting process, below are several fixed monthly expense categories. Write in the amount that you spend each month on each.

Mortgage/Rent	$_____
Gas & Electric	$_____
Car Payment(s)	$_____
Food	$_____
Telephone	$_____
Insurance	$_____

After your fixed expenses have been budgeted, turn your attention to the "irregular" expenses. This area includes: first, those expenses that are certain but only occur once or twice a year (i.e., Christmas, clothing purchases, or vacations), and second, those which might not occur at all in some years but still need to be budgeted (i.e., auto repairs, home maintenance, or uninsured medical expenses). These are the expenses that are usually neglected and which often cause discouragement when they arise because you aren't prepared for them in advance. An important part of the budgeting process includes setting money aside to cover these irregular expenses.

It is best to plan for a certain amount in each irregular expense category and then break it down into a monthly amount in order to save it a little at a time. For example, if you usually spend $600 on Christmas, you should set aside $50 each month so you have the cash to spend when it's time to do your Christmas shopping. Similarly, if you average $300 per year on auto repairs, set aside $25 each month for this purpose. It is important to try to budget for all of these irregular expenses in order to avoid a financial crunch when they inevitably arise.

APPLY

In the space below, write the annual amounts you usually spend in each category, followed by the monthly amount that needs to be set aside for each.

Home Repairs	$_____/year	$_____/month
Auto Maintenance	$_____/year	$_____/month
Vacation	$_____/year	$_____/month
Clothing	$_____/year	$_____/month
Christmas	$_____/year	$_____/month

Once your fixed expenses and irregular expenses have been entered into the budget, you can start working on the discretionary items. These would include such things as dining out, entertainment, babysitters, and spending money. It is not possible to prudently arrive at these figures until the fixed and irregular expenses have been calculated because you won't know how much money is available for this area. The discretionary expenses tend to represent the wants rather than the needs, and as such they are a slightly lower priority than the other two categories. Therefore, the amount you have left for discretionary expenses is determined by the amount already allocated to the fixed and irregular expenses. Once you know how much you have left to work with, you can go ahead and divide the balance between these discretionary areas.

This is where it becomes important to prioritize because you might not have enough money left each month to do all the things you would like to do. For example, if your budget will allow $200 for discretionary expenses and you like to have $50 each week for spending money, then you've used your entire allotment. Conversely, if you like to have some spending money each week but you also want to go out to dinner twice a month at $50 each meal, you've limited your available spending money to $25 per week. Both are legitimate discretionary expenses, but you must prioritize and divide the remaining funds accordingly.

If we have developed a lifestyle that is appropriate based on our income, there will be sufficient money available for discretionary expenses, and we won't feel like we must eliminate leisure from our lifestyle. More important, when we do spend money for dinner out or pizza in, we'll be free from the guilt that so often plagues us when we spend money on leisure.

APPLY

In the space below please write the monthly amounts you usually spend in each category. If you aren't sure, enter an amount that you think would be appropriate.

Dining Out	$_____
Hobbies	$_____
Entertainment	$_____
Babysitters	$_____
Memberships	$_____
Subscriptions	$_____

I should remind you at this point that, before you budgeted your living expenses, you should have already provided for your giving, taxes, and saving. Also, your debt repayment is covered under the fixed expenses, so you have met all of the financial responsibilities that God has given you. Budgeting in this way will provide a great sense of freedom because you'll know that you are handling God's money in a way that is both responsible and faithful. Discretionary spending will be limited to an amount that you can truly afford.

Spending Decisions

When managing our monthly finances through the use of a budget, it is very helpful to maintain a long-term perspective. On a short-term basis I might not be excited about the idea of reducing my monthly dining-out budget to accelerate debt repayment. A long-term perspective, however, would encourage me to make this decision because it allows me to pay off my car loan in three years instead of five. The small sacrifice I make today will save me two years worth of car payments in the future. Once the car is paid off, not only can I return to my normal dining-out budget, but I have considerable monthly excess at my discretion. If I'm only focused on today, I might not make a decision that could be extremely beneficial in the long run.

REFLECT

Share an example of a short-term sacrifice you've made in order to achieve an important long-term objective.

_____

_____

_____

One of the significant benefits of budgeting is that it usually ends the process of money slipping through the cracks. At the end of each month, most folks have no idea where their money went — they only know that it is gone. There is no question that you will spend less if you plan your spending, and the objective is to minimize or eliminate the money that tends to disappear each month unaccounted for.

Let's look at a realistic example of the likely long-term cost of failing to budget. Assume that someone in their mid-30s with average income, over the course of a year, is allowing $1,000 to slip through the cracks. This works out to just over $80 per month.

If you are struggling with this "money-slipping-through-the-cracks" concept, take this quick quiz: Review your checking account statement from last month and total the amount withdrawn in cash from the automated teller machine. Write that amount at the top of a sheet of paper. Underneath, make a list of the exact purchases that this money was used for. The amount that you can't account for — which is usually most of it — is the money that has slipped through the cracks.

REFLECT

How frequently do you make cash withdrawals from the automated teller machine? How do you keep track of these withdrawals or what they are used for?

_____

_____

_____

_____

_____

Back to our example, let's assume that through the process of adhering to a monthly budget, this $1,000 per year is saved rather than spent. What long-term difference does it make? I'll forego using additional investment charts to reinforce the point, but suffice it to say that overspending $1,000 per year during this person's working lifetime could cost *$1,000 per month* in lost retirement income. I probably don't have to tell you that, for the vast majority of retirees, an extra thousand dollars each month would be the difference between just barely making ends meet and living very comfortably. Again, a long-term perspective is required in order to embrace this type of planning. Most folks that I've met who are struggling financially in retirement would gladly have budgeted to control their spending had they known the tremendous impact it would have had on their retirement. The problem, obviously, is that by the time we retire it is too late.

I've served in the financial industry long enough to know that, for those who have never tried budgeting, or for those who tried and had a bad experience, this step will be the most challenging to take. I want to encourage you in the strongest terms to move forward. Knowing that we will eventually be called to give an account to God for the way we handled His resources should provide sufficient motivation to begin this process. My prayer, though, is that you are persuaded to move forward because of the positive benefits of doing so. Obedience is not just an obligation — it is a great blessing. We don't have to keep a budget so we can tell God how we spent His money. We are called to plan for our own benefit. Our Father in heaven will bless our obedience.

COMMIT

If you haven't already done so, make a firm commitment to planning your monthly expenses by using a budget. Spend a few moments in prayer asking the Lord to give you the discipline and wisdom that is needed to be successful in this area.

Budgeting Tips

I want to conclude this chapter with some important tips on successful budgeting. You'll find that, especially during the first year of budgeting, there will be numerous revisions as you rearrange your priorities and fine-tune your spending in the fixed categories. Once you've been at it for awhile, however, you'll probably only need to make changes once or twice a year. The following concepts will be particularly helpful for those just getting started in the budgeting process.

1. YOUR BUDGET MUST BE WRITTEN. When folks who are struggling financially seek help and are asked if they keep a monthly budget, a common response is, "Not in writing...I kind of keep one in my head." Let's begin by agreeing that, for the majority of the population, a budget that is not kept in writing is not a budget at all. The budgeting process is, by definition, proactive. Simply knowing what most of our monthly bills are doesn't constitute having a budget. Remember that a budget is not just a list of expenses — it is a spending plan. A budget requires us to take our monthly income and proactively determine how much we want to allocate to each spending category. Budgeting is done *before* the fact.

REFLECT

Some budgeting systems simply encourage you to keep all of your bills and receipts and record them at the end of the month. What is the potential problem with this type of system (i.e., recording after-the-fact vs. planning before-the-fact)?

_____

_____

_____

_____

Since we are preplanning our spending, and we want to keep track of where each dollar goes, it is vitally important that our budget is in writing. Otherwise, it is just not possible to remember how much we had planned to spend in each category. Whether you use a spiral notebook or a computer program, make sure your budget is in black and white.

2. YOUR BUDGET MUST BE REALISTIC. This might sound painfully obvious but I always find it helpful to remind folks before they begin to make sure the figures they use are realistic. There is a reason why a first attempt at creating a written budget might result in using figures that are less than accurate. Money tends to be a bit tight for the average family. Every penny that comes in usually goes out the same month. When that is the case, there is usually some consumer debt that has accumulated as a result of not having any excess cash flow each month. In this situation, it is not unusual for this process to confirm what should have been obvious: There is a negative cash flow, that is, there is more being spent each month than is coming in.

If this is the situation you find yourself in — and I have been there — it can be a very discouraging thing to see in black and white. Remember that the first step to solving a problem is to identify the problem. At this point we know that spending will have to be reduced to at least get back to a break-even level. The only other alternative is to increase the income, which isn't always an option for everyone. In any case, the problem has been identified.

REFLECT
Knowing your own personality and temperament, how would you likely respond if your first attempt at drafting a budget indicated that you were spending more than you were earning?

_____

_____

_____

When your written budget indicates a negative monthly cash flow, there are only two possible approaches. Some folks will give thanks to the Lord for the budgeting process and their being confronted with the habit of overspending their income. They will resolve to eliminate the problem and will do whatever is necessary to correct their course. This is the desirable outcome.

The other approach is to stare at the written budget in disbelief. The range of emotions that follow usually includes confusion, then frustration, and finally, defiance. Within a matter of minutes this approach will lead you to convince yourself that the budget is wrong. "I don't spend that much," you'll protest, "that's ridiculous." At this point you might decide to forget the whole thing. Or you might take the more common road and start changing the numbers to make the budget balance to your income. This approach is dangerous because it continues to conceal the spending problem, just as was the result of not budgeting at all.

What does it look like when we start changing the numbers? Let's say that your gas and electric bill for the past six months has ranged from $100 to $130, and we are headed into winter, when the bill usually tends to be higher. At first you rightly budgeted $130, but then you reason, *That month was an aberration. There's no way I spend that much every month. It's probably more like $100 a month. If I can get the kids to stop leaving the lights on in every room of the house, I'll bet I can get it down to $80.* And so it goes. The correct amount of $130 is quickly changed to $80. The groceries category then gets reduced below the normal amount, followed by the telephone bill, and then whatever other entries need to be reduced in order to balance the budget. The budget is now balanced on paper, which might make you feel better, but the problem of overspending has simply been swept under the carpet. Needless to say, this is not good.

REFLECT

Share a situation in which you, or someone you know, experienced "denial" regarding their monthly spending habits. What was the result?

_____

_____

_____

_____

_____

When I suggest that the budget must be realistic, I mean that it must accurately reflect the actual amounts that we spend each month in the fixed categories. It is certainly permissible to try to reduce some of these expenses as part of the budgeting process, but these are usually the areas that are the most difficult to reduce. When reductions are needed, they usually come from the discretionary categories. My encouragement with regard to the fixed expenses is to use numbers that you know are accurate.

3. YOUR BUDGET SHOULD BE DRIVEN BY YOUR GOALS. We talked earlier about conflicting priorities, and how spending decisions we make in one category will require that we reduce spending in another. This is why it is so important that, as you begin the budgeting process, you have already identified your specific financial goals. If one of your highest-ranked goals is to have no consumer debt, that will affect the amount of money that you'll budget for discretionary items such as dining out or a favorite hobby.

If a married couple has set a goal for the wife to stay at home with the kids, they will be willing to make many short-term sacrifices in order to realize this dream. A family might decide to do without a major vacation one year in order to pay off the car, which will free additional monthly cash flow for next year. In the absence of setting the goal this decision would probably never have been made. On the other hand, the family vacation might be the most important goal for a particular family, in which case spending might be reduced in another area in order to make sure that a major vacation can be afforded. In either case, the decisions were easy to make because the goals were clearly laid out.

4. CONSIDER THE ENVELOPE SYSTEM. For those not familiar with the envelope system, it is simply a budgeting method that forces spending discipline in the discretionary and/or irregular expense categories. This process involves putting a predetermined amount of cash into various envelopes each month in order to ensure that only the budgeted amounts get spent in those particular categories, and to reserve money for bills that are paid less frequently than on a monthly basis. There are a number of budget categories that are ideally suited to the envelope system, and this is a great way to eliminate overspending.

REFLECT

For a person who struggles with spending discipline, how might limiting their discretionary spending to cash purchases help to improve their circumstances?

_____

_____

_____

_____

_____

When helping people get started with budgeting, I usually recommend that they stop using the automated teller machine, because most of the spending that can't be accounted for is usually traced to unplanned cash withdrawals. Spending money, or a cash allowance, is a legitimate part of the budget, but it is the area that is most often abused. As such, it is one category that is ideal for the envelope system. Let's assume that you've completed your budget and have allotted $100 for your spending money next month. (Note: This is the one category that does not have to be accounted for. I don't favor saving receipts and trying to account each month for our cash allowance. What is important is making sure we don't exceed the budgeted amount, not figuring out whether we spent it on bowling, chewing gum, or pizza.) Rather than going to the cash machine each week for a withdrawal, we would take out $100 at the beginning of the month and put it in an envelope marked "spending." Then we use it as we need it.

The beauty of the envelope system is its simplicity. If there is money in the envelope, we have it to spend. When the envelope is empty, we're done for the month. Surely, this system requires discipline, but so does the entire budgeting process. If on the 25th of the month we decide to rent a couple movies but we discover that the envelope is empty, going back to the cash machine is not the solution. We must commit to a spending amount that is appropriate and then exercise the discipline necessary to stay within our budget. In this case we would forego the movies until we had the cash available.

REFLECT

When you are out of cash and have a desire to spend money on a discretionary item, are you more likely to buy it anyway or to wait until cash is available?

_____

_____

There are times, however, when it is okay to move money from one envelope to another. For example, folks who work in an environment where a suit or shirt and tie is required might have a monthly dry-cleaning expense. This is a category for which an envelope would probably be used. The dry-cleaning bill might vary from month to month, and there are times when you might not use all of the money that was budgeted for that expense. Let's go back to our example on the 25th of the month in which the envelope used for spending money is empty and you want to rent a couple movies. If your dry cleaning is finished for the month and there is cash left over, it is certainly acceptable to use that money for the movie rental, in effect moving it from the dry-cleaning envelope to the cash-allowance envelope. An empty dry-cleaning envelope is not a problem because it will be replenished when the new month begins.

REFLECT

List below some of the discretionary spending categories in your budget that might be best funded using the envelope system.

_____

_____

_____

Envelopes are also useful for irregular expenses, such as auto insurance (if paid every six months rather than monthly), life insurance, medical co-pays, etc. If you have a bill that comes due every three months and you want to make sure you have the money in hand when the next one comes due, you can break it down to a monthly amount and put each installment in an envelope. When the bill comes, you simply deposit the cash and write a check. Some folks will object that this is too tedious. That might be true, but it is far preferable to receiving a quarterly bill for your life insurance and not having the money available to pay it.

For people who are on a relatively tight budget with very little room for error, I highly recommend this system. Most folks who start using this system love it, and many will swear by it. I've been using it for many years and have no plans to do otherwise. Some of the spending categories for which my family has individual envelopes include: auto insurance, life insurance, homeowner's insurance, dry cleaning, oil changes, Jim's spending, Lori's spending, and family dates. When we were saving for a new swing set and wanted to teach the kids about making short-term sacrifices for a longer-term objective, we created a swing set envelope. When our family was praying and saving for a new puppy, we had a puppy envelope. This is not only a very practical way of handling discretionary and irregular expenses, it is also an excellent training tool for children.

A common objection to using the envelope system, especially for the irregular expenses such as auto insurance where the money might accumulate for up to six months, is that this money should be kept in an interest-bearing account rather than held in cash. I did a calculation once to determine how much interest income was lost over the course of a year by holding the money for irregular expenses in envelopes rather than in a savings account. The answer was around $10, much less than we might have expected. Of course, it is perfectly acceptable to use your savings account rather than envelopes for some of these categories. It is the process and discipline that are most important.

REFLECT

List one specific benefit that you think would result from using the envelope system. Then list one obstacle that might hinder you from using it.

Benefit: _____

Obstacle: _____

5. CONSIDER THE "BOMB-SHELTER" BUDGET. When outlining the specific steps involved in completing a budget worksheet I put them in the following order: fixed expenses, irregular expenses, and discretionary spending. We need to recognize that many folks, especially when they first start the budgeting process, may not have the luxury of funding all of these categories.

Most of us have struggled financially at one time or another. During such difficult times, the last thing we are concerned about in March is reserving money for Christmas in December. We're still trying to figure out how to pay the mortgage and the grocery bill each month. For folks in this situation I usually begin with what I refer to as the "bomb-shelter" budget. This budget is, by design, more defensive than proactive. It acknowledges that the amount of income being received each month is barely enough to make ends meet. In this case we are strategically allocating the scarce resources in order to make the money stretch as far as it possibly can.

If this is your situation, you will still use the same budget worksheet, but you will only complete the categories that are absolutely necessary. For example, you would still budget for such things as rent/mortgage, food, telephone service, and utilities, but you would not be able to reserve money for clothing, auto repairs, home maintenance, or Christmas. I'm not minimizing the importance of reserving money for these irregular expenses, but simply acknowledging that for many people this is not currently an option. At this point a reminder might be helpful. God is the Owner of all things, and God promises to provide for the needs of His children (Psalm 37:25; Philippians 4:19). If you are struggling financially but are being a faithful steward over the resources that God has entrusted to your care, you can rest assured that your Father in heaven will continue to provide for all of your needs. When your car breaks down and you haven't been able to reserve funds for auto repair, God will provide the repairs through some other means. When Christmas comes around and there is no excess cash because you've been diligently applying all of your income to other budgeting necessities, the Lord will provide for Christmas in some other way.

I've witnessed numerous instances of folks honoring the Lord with their income even though it was barely enough to meet their basic needs, and when the car breaks down an envelope of cash is anonymously given. Many churches have benevolence funds that exist for this specific purpose. I know many people who have the spiritual gift of giving, folks who are constantly on the lookout for faithful people in need. God provides for the needs of His people, and He often does it through others in the body of Christ. When we exercise faithful stewardship even during the trying times, we open ourselves to God's provision through channels other than our regular monthly income.

REFLECT

Share an experience in which God provided for your material needs through some means other than your own income.

_____

_____

_____

If you are going through a particularly difficult financial time right now, start with the bomb-shelter budget. Use the following worksheet as a guide and simply eliminate the categories that don't apply or that you cannot afford at the present time. Try to give some amount, no matter how small, to the Lord's work each month. Likewise, try to save something, even if it is so small an amount as to seem insignificant. Both of these actions represent wise stewardship according to God's Word, so it is important to try to do both and then allocate the rest to your monthly budget.

Some people need to use the bomb-shelter budget, some use the full, detailed budget, and many use something in between. Regardless of the amount of income that we have, remember that we are all held equally accountable to God for our stewardship of these resources. Keeping a written budget for the purpose of planning and controlling our spending will help to ensure that we are handling God's money in God's way.

STUDY QUESTIONS

1. What three types of living expenses that make up a typical budget were discussed? Give at least one example of each.

_____

_____

_____

2. What is one of the dangers of relying on cash withdrawals from the automated teller machine to fund your discretionary expenses?

_____

_____

_____

3. Name the five budgeting tips that were explained in this chapter.

_____

_____

_____

_____

_____

4. What are the two common responses when the budgeting process uncovers a negative monthly cash flow?

_____

_____

_____

5. Briefly explain the envelope system, and name several budget categories for which it might be useful.

_____

_____

_____

6. What steps will you take to begin implementing the recommendations made in this section on budgeting?

_____

_____

Sample Budget

	MONTHLY	ANNUAL	TOTAL
HOUSING			
Mortgage			
Insurance			
Maintenance & Repairs			
Home Improvements			
Furnishings			
Property Tax			
Maid Service			
UTILITIES			
Electricity			
Gas			
Water/Sanitation			
Telephone			
Cell Phone			
FOOD			
Groceries/Products			
Vitamins/Supplements			
CLOTHING			
Husband			
Wife			
Children			
TRANSPORTATION			
Car Payments			
Gas/Oil			
Auto Insurance			

License/Tag _____ _____ _____
Maintenance/Repair _____ _____ _____

ENTERTAINMENT
Dining Out _____ _____ _____
Trips/Vacations _____ _____ _____
Baby-sitters _____ _____ _____
Memberships _____ _____ _____
Books/Films/Tapes _____ _____ _____
Entertaining/Parties _____ _____ _____
Cable TV _____ _____ _____

MEDICAL
Doctor _____ _____ _____
Dentist _____ _____ _____
Therapist _____ _____ _____
Drugs/Medicine _____ _____ _____
Medical Insurance Premium _____ _____ _____

INSURANCE
Life - Husband _____ _____ _____
Life - Wife _____ _____ _____
Life - Children _____ _____ _____
Disability _____ _____ _____
Long-term Care _____ _____ _____

CHILDREN
Lessons _____ _____ _____
Allowances _____ _____ _____
Activities _____ _____ _____
Lunches _____ _____ _____

GIFTS

    Christmas   _____ _____ _____

    Anniversary   _____ _____ _____

    Birthdays   _____ _____ _____

    Weddings   _____ _____ _____

MISCELLANEOUS

    Beauty Salon/Barber   _____ _____ _____

    Laundry/Dry Cleaning   _____ _____ _____

    Subscriptions   _____ _____ _____

    Cash Allowance - Husband   _____ _____ _____

    Cash Allowance - Wife   _____ _____ _____

    Postage/Shipping   _____ _____ _____

    Pets   _____ _____ _____

    Other   _____ _____ _____

EDUCATION

    Private School   _____ _____ _____

    College   _____ _____ _____

    Homeschooling   _____ _____ _____

TOTAL EXPENSES   _____ _____ _____

AVERAGE MONTHLY EXPENDITURES   _____

-12-
DEBT REDUCTION
PART 1

"For the LORD your God will bless you as he has promised, and you will lend to many nations but will borrow from none."

—Moses, Deuteronomy 15:6

"The rich rule over the poor, and the borrower is servant to the lender."

—King Solomon, Proverbs 22:7

I watched as they ran playfully across the beach, laughing and holding hands like high-school sweethearts. Bodies firm and tan, faces beaming with joy, alone together in an unnamed tropical paradise, renewing their relationship far away from the pressures of everyday life. A perfect picture that draws us in and leaves us longing to share such a moment with the one we love. And then the point is made. A small symbol appears at the bottom of the television screen, barely noticeable to the conscious mind. It is the logo of a major credit-card company, quietly reminding us that all of this beauty and fun can be ours today.

Having counseled many people who were distraught and in anguish over a debt load that had grown to a level that threatened financial ruin, I've often marveled at the portrait of borrowing that is painted by purveyors of consumer debt. It makes sense, however, to portray credit-card debt in this positive light. Why would they depict a more realistic example of a family that reaches for the credit card every time their material appetites need to be satisfied?

Picture a different television commercial for the same company and starring the same couple. This time, their faces are more intense and their eyes tired and cold. Seated at the dining-room table, she watches quietly as he totals the stack of bills that are before him. He sighs heavily. Having no cash on hand, he nervously glances at the calendar for the fourth time to confirm the specific day of his next paycheck.

Their credit cards are all at their borrowing limit, and several of the bills were due two weeks ago. Ironically, at the very time this couple was relaxing on the beach, a major storm was moving through their hometown, and the basement was being flooded once again. They had discussed waterproofing the basement the last time this happened, but there was no money to do it and their available credit had been committed to the tropical vacation. Here they sit, frustrated and angry, the silence broken only by the steady ticking of the grandfather clock.

I'm not a marketing expert by any means, but I would guess that this advertisement, though more realistic, might not be good for the credit-card business! Yet most of us identify much more readily with the scene at the dining-room table than the one on the beach. It is easy to understand why consumer debt has become such a significant problem for us today. We've already discussed our fleshly desire for instant gratification. We want to be happy and fulfilled, and we continually fall into the trap of believing that more stuff will satisfy that desire. Even committed Christians who sincerely desire to honor God with their resources are not immune from clever marketing schemes. We understand intellectually that Christ alone can fill the void in our souls, but the flesh longs for something more tangible. When the pressures of daily life start to build, we look once again to the things of this world to provide relief.

REFLECT

Describe an advertisement you've seen recently that encourages the use of consumer debt by appealing to the flesh.

_____

_____

_____

_____

_____

From a practical-application standpoint, this might be the most important chapter in this book. In the vast majority of cases, folks who are struggling financially can trace their problems to the misuse of consumer debt. If there is someone out there who can encourage you in this area it is probably me. Not because I'm smarter than those reading this book; on the contrary, I've probably made more mistakes, and spent to greater extremes, than all but the most hardened materialists. It is because I've made the same mistakes that I can provide counsel and encouragement to those in this position.

I am not someone who looks down on those in debt, self-righteously chastising them for their indiscretion and smugly affirming that their problems are deserved. Rather, I grieve for those caught in the trap of debt because I know intimately how it happens and how it feels. I have spent countless evenings sitting at the dining-room table, listening to the silence as I struggled to find a way to pay the bills. I've spent money that I didn't have to buy things I didn't need, and then juggled various credit lines to make payments that I couldn't afford. Like many of you, I've lived through those times when I dreaded the telephone's ringing because I knew it was one of my many creditors trying to collect a debt that I had no money to repay. I struggle with my own emotions as I write this chapter because I have known the intense pain caused by the trap of debt. I desire with all my heart to be an encouragement to those reading this and to see all of us freed from the bondage of excessive debt.

What Is Debt?

Let me begin by defining what debt is *not*. Contrary to popular belief and occasional teaching, debt is not a sin. It might at times be a bad idea, or a symptom of a deeper problem, but it is not a sin to borrow money. Debt doesn't become sin until we refuse, or fail, to repay it. When I suggest that biblical references to debt are generally negative, understand that the Bible isn't referring to all instances of borrowing or credit. A general definition of the term *debt* might include owing money to anyone, regardless of the circumstances. For purposes of this chapter, however, my use of the term *debt* refers to borrowed money that we have no currently available means to repay, or no intention to repay. Some of the biblical references in this chapter will apply to all forms of borrowing, but several will be more applicable to this specific definition.

REFLECT

List below at least five common types of debt.

1. _____

2. _____

3. _____

4. _____

5. _____

We probably don't need to spend much time on the concept of borrowing money that you have no intention of repaying. I think we can all agree that this is sin. The most common example of this practice occurs when someone is planning to file for bankruptcy in order to have their debts eliminated. Before hiring a bankruptcy attorney they go on a spending spree, taking all of their credit cards up to the borrowing limit. Then they successfully have these debts eliminated by a bankruptcy judge.

It boggles the mind that our society has come to the place where irresponsible, and even deceitful, spending can be rewarded by simply asking a judge to forgive all of one's debt. Alas, that has become the usual strategy for folks who enjoy spending recklessly. I was quite surprised years ago when a local Christian attorney actually advised a client to take this approach. The woman being counseled had no money to pay for the attorney's advice, so she was advised to use a credit card to pay his fee of several thousand dollars and then have the debt dismissed in bankruptcy. Thankfully, she sought a second opinion.

Presuming upon God

Borrowing without having a sure means of repayment, on the other hand, can be a bit of a gray area. If someone borrows money intending not to repay, the sin is clear. But what about the woman who borrows to buy a car knowing that her employment income is more than sufficient to make the payments, but then her job is eliminated unexpectedly and she is temporarily without income? Has she sinned? Although some might argue the strict position that she sinned by presuming upon the future, there are circumstances in which I would be inclined to defend her decision. Let's assume that this has been a stable job and she has gotten consistently positive performance reviews. Her experience is such that her services will most likely be in demand even if she were to leave her employment, whether voluntarily or otherwise. Assume further that there was no way of predicting that the company would decide to merge with a competitor and eliminate a number of positions. I would argue that, on the surface at least, her decision was sound and presumption was not an issue.

If all extensions of credit were classified as sinful presumption, we would have to cancel even our gas and electric service because using it presumes upon next month's income. Our local utility extends credit to us by providing the service before payment is made. After we've consumed the service and the meter is read, we get a bill that requires payment several weeks later. If I tend toward a strict legal interpretation of the concept of "presuming upon God," then I am sinning when I turn on the heat or air conditioning not knowing for certain that I'll have a job next month when the bill comes due. Of course, it is entirely possible to make purchases on credit that would constitute presumption, but I think there are many cases of borrowing that do not violate this biblical principle.

REFLECT

Give an example of borrowing that you would classify as presuming upon God or the future.

_____

_____

_____

When does borrowing become presumptuous? Let's take the example of a young Christian man with an inconsistent work history. He has bounced from job to job, never earning much more than minimum wage and having refused a number of opportunities to acquire marketable skills. The longest he has ever held a job is seven months. He has been in financial trouble several times due to credit-card debt and has always relied on his parents to bail him out. They've made it clear that he is now on his own. He likes the beach, and when he received an offer to purchase a time share in Ocean City, he went ahead and signed the note. He had to pay 21.99 percent interest on the loan due to his short time on the job and a few late payments in his credit history, but he loved the idea of having his own place at the beach. When challenged by a friend at church regarding his spending money that he didn't have, he arrogantly quoted Philippians 4:19 and assured his friend that God promises to provide for all of his needs.

I think it is safe to say that this time share purchase probably falls into the sin category of presuming upon God. Even if his currently earned income was sufficient to handle the monthly payment, his lack of work ethic and history of losing jobs makes it unlikely that he'll be able to honor this long-term obligation. I purposely selected an extreme example to make my point, but most cases of borrowing will fall between the two extremes. That is why I referred to this as a gray area. There aren't many hard-and-fast rules I can give you that will apply in all cases. We must consider our heart motivation for the purchase we're considering, the economic implications of borrowing, and the likelihood of our being able to repay.

REFLECT

What sins are at the heart of a Christian's tendency to continually use consumer debt to purchase the things they want but can't afford?

_____

_____

_____

_____

One way to avoid the sin of presumption when using credit is to borrow only for tangible assets that secure the loan and to make a sufficient down payment to eliminate the risk to the lender. For example, if I borrow money for a trip to Europe and then lose my job and am unable to make the payments, all of that money is at risk to the lender. If I borrow to buy a car, however, and put 40 percent down while financing the balance, the risk to my creditor is dramatically reduced, if not totally eliminated. The car itself provides collateral for the loan and, even if I should find myself unable to make the payments, the lender can repossess the car and sell it at auction. Because I made a large down payment and borrowed only 60 percent of the car's value, the lender is almost certain to recover his money even if I should default.

A similar example of borrowing without presumption involves the zero-percent financing that many car dealers have been offering during the economic downturn. Many Christians who have saved sufficient funds to pay cash for their next car are choosing to leave that money invested and use the attractive financing instead. They are not presuming upon the Lord because, not only does the car itself provide collateral for the loan, but they also have the funds available to repay the debt at any time.

There is certainly a biblical admonition against presuming upon the Lord, and we need to avoid violating this principle. But it should not be assumed that absolutely all uses of credit are in violation of this biblical principle. There will always be cases in which we can use credit while still remaining faithful in our stewardship of God's resources. If you are considering a purchase involving some amount of debt and you aren't quite sure if your decision is wise and consistent with God's teaching, it is best to seek counsel from a mature Christian.

REFLECT

Are you accustomed to seeking counsel from a mature Christian when considering a major purchase? If so, give an example of one such experience and the decision that resulted.

_____

_____

_____

Three Dangers of Debt

The focal point of my discussion on debt will be confined to the area of consumer debt such as credit cards, signature loans, and, in some cases, home equity lines of credit. The reason is that the majority of individuals and families who are struggling financially can trace their problems directly to the misuse or abuse of consumer debt. Although we can certainly overspend on a home or a car, the damage is more limited due to the fixed term of the loan.

As an example, if I take a three-year loan to purchase a late-model used car, the monthly payment may be higher than I can comfortably afford, and I might even struggle at times to make the payments. But I know for certain that, at the end of three years, the loan will be repaid. Although the term is much longer, the same principle holds true for my home mortgage. Most consumer debt, however, doesn't have a specific repayment term. We can make our monthly payments faithfully year after year and never put a significant dent in the original amount borrowed.

REFLECT

Share an experience (if applicable) in which you have spent years making monthly payments on consumer debt without significantly reducing the loan amount.

_____

_____

_____

The most obvious danger we face with consumer debt is simply borrowing a larger amount than we can afford. This is rarely intentional; the amount of consumer debt that we accumulate tends to sneak up on us. Like the proverbial frog placed in a kettle of water that is brought to a boil, our monthly debt payments often increase so slowly that we don't realize we have a problem until it is too late. I've observed over the years three particular areas in which consumer debt can become hazardous to our financial health: the credit-card "comfort zone"; the minimum-payment syndrome; and lost opportunity. Let's explore each debt trap in greater detail.

Credit-Card "Comfort Zone"

For those not familiar with the concept of a "comfort zone," the best analogy is to think about a typical thermostat. If you want to keep your home or apartment at a temperature of seventy-two degrees you will set the thermostat at precisely that setting. If the internal mechanism were perfectly precise, your heat or air conditioner would be constantly turning on and off, adjusting immediately each time the room temperature moved even slightly off the target setting. In reality, there is a certain comfort zone that keeps the unit from constant activity. During the winter your heater, although the thermostat is set at seventy-two degrees, will not actually turn on until the room cools a couple of degrees below the target. Likewise, the heat will not shut off until the temperature has risen a couple of degrees above that setting. Your ideal room temperature might be seventy-two degrees, but the thermostat responds by creating a comfort zone between seventy and seventy-four degrees. The heating unit will only respond when the temperature is above or below the comfort zone.

How does this relate to consumer debt? I would like to propose that we all have a particular comfort zone with regard to the amount of consumer debt we are comfortable carrying. Someone might protest, "No way, Jim. I never carry credit-card debt." If that's true of you, it doesn't mean that you don't have a comfort zone, it just means that your target setting is zero. My hope in this chapter is that all of our credit-card comfort zones will move steadily toward zero. The fact is, however, that most of us are quite comfortable carrying some level of credit-card debt. That amount for each person will vary depending on several factors, not the least of which is your annual income. A family with an annual income of $30,000 will probably have a lower comfort zone than the family earning $75,000.

REFLECT

What amount of debt would you say represents the upper limit of your credit-card comfort zone?

Let's assume that your comfort zone is $3,000 in credit-card debt. At that level the monthly payment is probably around $70 or so, an affordable amount for most folks carrying this level of debt. Imagine a period in which you incur a number of irregular expenses, both expected and unexpected. Perhaps you have some car maintenance that can't be delayed any longer, followed by a plumbing emergency. Then your summer vacation comes along, and most of that ends up getting added to your credit card. Suddenly your total amount of credit-card debt has increased to $3,900. You start to get very uncomfortable because this is about as high as it has ever been.

In this situation you will likely resolve to avoid using the card until the debt is reduced to a more manageable level. You start making more than the minimum monthly payment, adding another $25 or $30 each month as you are able, but it doesn't seem to be making a significant difference in the outstanding balance. A few months later, as the weather begins to turn cold, you find out your heat pump isn't working. Frustration turns to anger at the unfortunate timing. Having no cash for the much-needed repair, you have no choice but to charge it. The repair is major, and your debt has now climbed to $4,500. You almost lose control when your spouse asks about Christmas shopping, and you are starting to lose sleep at night because your monthly payment has increased to $105 and you don't know how to get this debt under control.

REFLECT

Share an example (if applicable) of a time when you relied too heavily on credit cards to fund a series of expenses, causing you to exceed your comfort zone. How did you respond?

_____

_____

_____

This is the point at which you will do almost anything to start reducing the debt; the top end of your comfort zone has been violated. You'll work overtime and be willing to eliminate most of your discretionary spending. You'll start carrying a brown bag to work rather than eating lunch out. Any bonus or tax refund will go directly to paying down the credit card. If the problem is severe enough you might even take a temporary or second job to accelerate repayment. Almost everyone who uses credit cards with regularity has had this experience. In this case, the debt thermostat is set at $3,000, and we've discovered that the top end of the comfort zone is $4,500. That is helpful to know, but it doesn't begin to solve the problem. We might be encouraged by the aggressive manner in which the problem is being attacked, but let's consider what happens as the debt starts to get reduced.

After four months of working fifty-five hour weeks, you have earned enough in overtime pay to reduce the credit card debt to $2,500. You are starting to feel exhausted so you go back to your normal work schedule, content with your handling of what felt like a financial crisis. Then you get a tax refund of $400. You aren't in the spending mood so you add that amount to the credit-card bill. While cleaning out the garage you decide to go ahead and sell a few pieces of furniture that are just taking up space. Another $200 is received, after which you get an unexpected $400 bonus check. You've been in the habit of using all excess income to reduce debt, and you do so with this additional income as well. You aren't thinking about the results until you get your credit-card bill and notice that the balance is down to $1,500. This is great! You haven't seen it that low in years. You have a great sense of satisfaction, knowing that this debt had reached a peak just six short months ago. Now your system shuts down, identifying the lower end of your comfort zone at $1,500.

REFLECT

What amount of debt defines the lower end of your credit-card comfort zone?

_____

_____

_____

One might think that in this scenario you would get excited that total repayment is within reach. But it will never occur to you. Why? Because you've never set a goal to pay it off, and, frankly, you've always carried some level of credit-card debt. It just seems normal. You are certainly pleased that the balance is down to $1,500, but further acceleration is not even a consideration. Within a few months, the way you think about the credit-card debt will begin to change. Remember that your thermostat is set to $3,000. This is the amount you are accustomed to carrying, and the monthly payment at that level is easily affordable. Two things will happen. One is that you will start to look at making some major purchases, and the other is that you will feel like you have $1,500 of cash available to spend. Why $1,500? Because that is the difference between your current amount of credit-card debt and your thermostat. It is almost certain that in several months time your credit-card balance will be back to $3,000. And it won't bother you in the least.

This is the problem with the credit-card comfort zone; it tends to work in both directions. When consumer debt is too high, our repayment system is engaged, and we begin to use all possible means to reduce the debt. When the debt level is too low, however, the system is activated in the other direction, and we'll make sure that we spend until normalcy is restored. You'll see in the following section why the credit-card comfort zone is such a danger, especially when we can only afford to make the minimum payments.

REFLECT

Share an example from your past in which a dramatic reduction in your credit-card debt led you to increase spending until the amount of credit-card debt returned to a more "normal" level.

_____

_____

_____

_____

_____

_____

A particular risk with the credit-card comfort zone is the ease with which it can eventually increase. In the example I gave above, it only took six months after the top of the zone was violated to bring the debt all the way down to the bottom end. In real life we aren't always as successful. We'll still go through the same process of working hard to bring the debt level back to within our comfort zone, but what would have happened if several more unexpected repairs had surfaced in rapid succession? Now you are working diligently to repay the debt, but it is still growing more quickly than you can eliminate it. If you aren't careful, your sanity will demand that you change your expectation and increase your target setting. We don't like to feel defeated or hopeless. Once we give in and accept that we can't get the debt paid down to our desired level, we are prone to move our comfort zone up a few degrees. Our target setting moves from $3,000 to $5,000 and the cycle continues.

My purpose in spending so much time on this concept is that, in my estimation, it is the most basic reason that so many of us are struggling with an unmanageable level of consumer debt. It is rarely one particular purchase that we can point to as having caused the problem. It is the combination of planned purchases, impulse spending, and emergency repairs, all accumulating over a long period of time. Those who experience it often feel like a drowning victim. They are treading water and starting to feel out of breath. They realize that they need to get back to shore, but the tide is pulling them out. A sense of panic begins, and they start swimming with all of their might against the tide that is gradually pulling them farther out to sea. Their desperate gasps for air bring them a mouthful of salt water. They feel themselves going under....

There are numerous financial challenges that a person can face, but being suffocated by an excessive debt load is among the most painful. Now that we understand the concept of the credit-card comfort zone, let us immediately resolve to reduce our target setting to zero. Our goal is to work diligently and faithfully to eliminate our consumer debt, all the while focusing on maintaining it at zero after it is paid off. Once accomplished, we will truly be on the road to financial freedom.

REFLECT

If credit-card debt is a concern, what steps can you take immediately in order to reduce your credit-card comfort zone?

_____

_____

_____

Minimum-Payment Syndrome

I remember getting my first credit card. What power! It was 1981, and one of my friends had applied for, and received, a credit card from a local department store at which we both enjoyed shopping. (It had a great sporting goods department!) I decided to apply also, and within thirty days the shiny new card came in the mail. Being a firm believer in patriotism and capitalism, I immediately did what any red-blooded American would have done: I went right to the store and bought a bunch of stuff I didn't need!

I can still remember the thrill of walking into a store with no cash and walking out with some new clothes and sports equipment. I can't remember exactly what I bought, but the bill came out to around $250. I should mention that I did have the cash in my checking account to pay for this stuff, but I wanted to try out my new credit card. I figured the store would send me a bill at some point, and then I would just write them a check to cover the purchase. But a strange thing happened three weeks later when I received my first credit-card statement.

I had not seen one of these before so I scrutinized it in great detail, including the small print on the back. What motivated my close review of the statement was that there appeared to be a glaring mistake on the front. The top section seemed correct, showing the date I was in the store and detailing each item that I purchased. At the bottom of the right-hand column was the total cost of my shopping excursion: $250. The problem was at the bottom of the page. There was a payment coupon with a perforated edge and the words, "Please return this portion with your payment." It was on this payment coupon that the error seemed to occur. There was an empty box for me to write the amount of my payment, and under this box there was an indication that the amount due was $10. *How could I only owe them $10?* I thought. I looked back to the top of the statement and confirmed once again that they had accounted for every item purchased. I was confused.

REFLECT

Why do you think the minimum monthly payments on most credit cards are so low?

_____

_____

When I glanced back at the payment coupon, things became a bit clearer. The actual wording was, "Minimum Payment Due: $10." Not being the brightest twenty-one-year-old in town, I had to read the fine print on the back to figure out why there was a minimum payment. The statement made it clear that I had a choice. I could pay the outstanding balance in full whenever I wanted, but I could also choose instead to make a minimum payment each month, which in this case amounted to only $10. Imagine what was going through the mind of this budding materialist. I have all of this stuff that I just bought, and I get to keep it. I have the cash to pay for it, and I get to keep that too. And these fine folks are telling me that if I just send along ten dollars each month, everyone will be happy. I was like a kid in a candy store!

I decided almost immediately that I preferred the minimum payment option but, being somewhat financially inclined, I did find myself wondering how long it might take to repay the debt. I studied this section of small print intently. The payment was calculated by simply taking one of two numbers, either a percentage of the total outstanding balance or ten dollars, whichever was greater. I did a quick calculation and determined that if I decided to make only the minimum payments until the balance was paid in full, it would have taken between two and three years to pay off the debt. Further study indicated that this was common practice back in the early 1980s. The minimum payment option was usually designed in such a way as to make sure the term of the debt was three years or less.

REFLECT

If you use a credit card today to make a major purchase, and you are only able to afford to make the minimum monthly payments, how long do you think it will take to repay the entire balance?

Several years ago I was preparing to teach a workshop on family finances and I planned to share this example. In order to ensure accuracy, I decided to repeat my calculation using the minimum payment terms of several of the country's largest credit-card companies. I was shocked by my findings, realizing that the terms of consumer debt have changed radically over the past two decades. I'll illustrate with a real example from an ad in this weekend's newspaper.

Let's pretend that your TV is getting old and you decide it's time to get a new one. You begin shopping and the large-screen TV really catches your eye. It costs more than you had planned to spend, but it is on sale, and if you get the store's credit card, they'll provide free delivery. This works out perfectly because your other credit card is close to the limit, so you'll need a new one in order to buy the more expensive TV. The interest rate of 19.8 percent looks a bit high, but the monthly payment is only $36. Your budget has been tight of late so you won't be able to pay more than the minimum payments, but you feel comfortable that you can afford it. Question: Assuming you make only the minimum payments, how long do you think it will take to pay off the TV? Answer: Thirty-nine years and four months. Friend, your house will be paid off before the TV!

REFLECT

What was your reaction to this example? Do you think most people understand the result of making only the minimum monthly payments?

_____

_____

_____

_____

When I said earlier that consumer debt tends to sneak up on us, this is what I mean. We don't go into this type of purchase thinking, _Gee, only forty years and this thing will be paid for!_ We have no idea how long it will take because our marketing culture has long since taught us to think of spending, not in terms of overall cost, but whether we can afford the monthly payment.

When is the last time you bought a car and had the finance manager talk about the total cost of the vehicle? The more common discussion revolves around the monthly payment that you can afford. This is true whether buying a car, a house, or a big-screen TV. If we can handle the monthly payment, we think we can afford the purchase. In this particular case the advertisement failed to mention that, if you took advantage of the special financing, this $1,800 TV would cost $8,493.46 by the time it was paid for!

Without getting into unnecessary technical detail, let me try to explain briefly why it takes so long to repay consumer debt. A typical minimum payment calculation is based on some percentage of the outstanding balance, often 2 percent. Once that calculation falls below a certain amount, say $10 a month, the higher amount will apply until the debt is repaid. The interest rate in this purchase is 19.8 percent annually, which equates to 1.65 percent per month. The fact is that you are making a payment of 2 percent each month, of which the first 1.65 percent is being applied to interest charges. Only the remaining .35 percent is available to reduce your outstanding balance. In other words, *over 82 percent of every payment goes to interest.* No wonder we make payment after payment and never see the principal amount substantially reduced. Even so, if the monthly payment remained a flat amount such as we have with our car loan and mortgage, the debt would be repaid in less time.

The biggest problem with making the minimum monthly payment is that as the loan balance declines, so does the minimum payment. Even though the monthly percentages remain constant, the amount being applied to principal each month is in decline because the minimum payment drops each time some principal is repaid. This is probably more detail than most folks care to read, but it is very important to understand how the system works in order to protect ourselves the next time we are contemplating a major purchase.

REFLECT

Based on what has been covered so far in this chapter, what behavioral changes (if any) do you anticipate making with regard to the use of credit cards?

_____

_____

Before moving on to the next topic, let us consider the impact of the credit-card comfort zone on the minimum-payment syndrome. As I mentioned, we don't consciously decide to buy a TV that will take us forty years to repay. We have every intention of paying it off as we're able. The problem is that we've become so accustomed to making this monthly payment, we eventually stop thinking of it as a debt. It simply becomes lumped in with our electric bill and phone bill, just another monthly outflow for which we need to budget. Although we might go through periods of accelerating our consumer-debt payments, as will happen when the balances exceed our credit-card comfort zone, the existence of some credit-card debt over the long term is all but assured. Fifteen years from now we might have actually paid enough on the credit card to pay off the TV, but that debt has since been replaced by something else, perhaps a new recliner or a vacation. The result is that we spend our working lifetime diverting increasing amounts of monthly cash flow to interest payments on debt that never goes away. That habit leads to the third danger with consumer debt, the opportunity lost.

Total Cost Equals Opportunity Lost

This is the side of the debt equation that escapes most of us unless we happen to work in the financial industry. Understanding this concept will not only save you tens of thousands of dollars in interest charges, it could earn you hundreds of thousands of dollars toward your retirement goals. Let me explain.

REFLECT

To what extent do you think most people with credit-card debt ever consider the long-term consequences of this debt?

Let's continue with our assumption that your credit-card comfort zone is $3,000 over the next twenty years. The total amount of debt fluctuates over time but it usually gravitates back toward this amount. Let's further assume that you've been diligent to always pay more than the minimum requirement, say $100 per month on average vs. the $60 minimum, and the interest rate on the card is 16.99 percent. With apologies to those who have an intense disdain for mathematical word problems, what is the total cost of carrying this debt? The annual interest cost is $509.70 ($3,000 x 16.99 percent) and the total interest over twenty years is $10,194 ($509.70 x 20). The typical response to this question is that the total cost of this comfort zone is $13,194 ($10,194 interest plus repayment of the $3,000 loan). If you are like me, this really doesn't sound like that big of a deal. I mean, $10,000 is a lot of money, but that amount over twenty years just doesn't seem like it will lead many families into financial ruin. If this was the only cost of carrying this credit-card debt, I probably wouldn't have been motivated to write this chapter.

We are missing the most important part of the calculation, however. Let's assume that this book arrived in your hands just in the nick of time. You've embraced the concepts in this chapter and resolved to eliminate all credit-card debt within the year. As a result, you will actually be able to save and invest that $100 per month for the next twenty years rather than use it for debt payments. You select a highly rated growth mutual fund with a long-term track record that has averaged 12 percent annual return since inception. Your $100 per month invested at a 12 percent rate over the next twenty years will yield $99,915. This is the cost of the opportunity that has been lost by continuing to carry the debt. Therefore, whereas the total principal plus interest cost for this credit-card comfort zone is only $13,194 after twenty years, the total cost is actually $113,109! This figure is derived by adding the opportunity cost to the total interest and principal repayment.

What is the cost in retirement? It could be as much as $800 per month for the rest of your life, a very attractive supplemental income for most retirees. Consider a credit-card comfort zone of $5,000 or $7,000, which levels are becoming increasingly common, and you can see that the opportunity cost will quickly accumulate to hundreds of thousands of dollars after twenty years. Even if you are already headed toward financial independence in retirement because of the quality of your employer's retirement plan, eliminating your credit-card comfort zone will provide significant assets to be used for giving to the Lord's work or leaving an inheritance for the kids. When making a purchase on credit, be it furniture, major appliances, clothes, or vacations, let's try to think in terms of the total cost of the purchase.

Many common financial mistakes could be avoided by simply having the necessary information in advance. Serious financial problems tend to result from behavioral problems much more than from our circumstances. The objective for this chapter was to help change the way we think about consumer debt. I hope this information will provide the motivation that is needed to improve our behavior with regard to spending and debt.

Now that we've "counted the cost" with regard to the excessive use of consumer debt, let's move on to the practical side of this discussion: debt elimination.

STUDY QUESTIONS

1. What did you learn in this chapter that was most surprising?

_____

_____

_____

2. Describe the credit-card "comfort zone" and how it affects spending.

_____

_____

_____

3. What is the "minimum-payment syndrome" and how can it be harmful?

_____

_____

_____

4. Explain the "opportunity cost" of consistently carrying consumer debt.

_____

_____

_____

-13-
DEBT REDUCTION
PART 2

"The wicked borrow and do not repay."

—King David, Psalm 37:21a

"You do not have, because you do not ask God. When you ask, you do not receive, because you ask with wrong motives."

—James, the brother of Jesus, James 4:2b-3

I'll take the liberty at this point to assume that those of us who have some level of consumer debt, regardless of the amount, have determined to do everything we can to eliminate this debt as quickly as possible. Whether it takes six months or six years, the only way to become free from the trap of consumer debt is to make a firm commitment to eliminate it completely. As we move forward with repayment, we must also consciously reduce our credit-card comfort zone to zero in order to ensure that, once paid off, we never have to deal with this issue again. We must start to see ourselves as wise stewards, who use credit cards for convenience only, always paying the bill in full at the end of the month.

Debt Elimination

Now let's turn our attention to some of the specific steps that can be taken to start paying off our consumer debt. Not all of these ideas will work for everyone, but everyone should be able to use at least a few. If implementing one or more of these steps seems inconvenient, keep your eyes firmly focused on the end result. Once your credit-card debt is gone, your financial life will never be the same. You will begin to experience a sense of financial freedom that you've probably never known before. So let's be willing to make some short-term sacrifices for the sake of our long-term financial health.

1. BEGIN WITH PRAYER. I'm not trying to over-spiritualize our decision to repay our debts; I just want to begin by acknowledging that God alone is our provision. Just as He gives us an income and instructions for handling it, as Owner of everything, He is more than able to help us resolve our debt problems. The starting point in this process is to repent of any sin of which we're aware that has led to the accumulation of excessive debt and to ask God for His grace and mercy in turning things around. If you are resting in Jesus Christ, remember that you are a son or daughter of almighty God. You are not an orphan. Often when we sin we are reluctant to go back to our Father and ask for help. But God delights to restore us when we've acknowledged our sin and come to Him helpless and broken.

DISCOVER

Write out Psalm 51:17. Then spend a moment in prayer repenting of any known sin in the area of your finances. Ask God to pour out His grace and mercy on you.

_____

_____

_____

_____

_____

_____

If you are a parent you will understand this truth. Although we are surely disappointed when our children disobey us, we stand ready to forgive and restore when they acknowledge their mistake and take responsibility for it. If that is true of human parents, how much more so is it true of our Father in heaven who is perfect in love and mercy?

So let's go to God consistently in prayer, asking Him to intervene in our difficult circumstances. As we walk forward in obedience, God will often provide additional resources with which to further accelerate our debt reduction. But let's take care to ask with proper motives and to use the resources He provides appropriately.

Read James 4:2-3. In asking God to increase our income, what would be an example of an improper motive? What would be a proper motive?

Improper: _____

Proper: _____

As you begin doing your part to repay this debt, and consistently pray that God will guide and help you, expect to see His faithfulness in the process. Make sure, however, that those additional resources that might become available to you are used for their intended purpose. The first step in the process of eliminating our debt is to pray.

2. PERFORM CARD SURGERY. You won't need a scalpel or a physician for this operation — a pair of sharp scissors will suffice. It is difficult to take this step of cutting our credit cards in half and disposing of them, but it is usually necessary. It is vitally important in this process to refuse to go any further into debt. We do that by making an absolute commitment to avoiding the continued use of debt, and this resolution is more easily accomplished if we remove the temptation by destroying the credit cards. Once this type of debt has become a problem for us, the credit cards themselves have become somewhat of a lifeline. We've forgotten how to trust God with our finances because we have the credit cards to bail us out when money is tight. The more dependent we've become on using our credit cards, the more difficult this action becomes. However, it can also be extremely liberating.

REFLECT

How did you respond to the idea of destroying your credit cards, even if they still have outstanding balances?

_____

_____

_____

_____

Some counselors will tell you to cut up every credit card in your wallet. Practicality leads me to take a slightly different approach. Our society seems at times to prefer credit cards to cash, and it would be extremely difficult to get by without any credit cards at all. Anyone who has tried to write a check for groceries understands the need to carry a major credit card. There are other important uses for credit cards that most of us wouldn't even think about unless we no longer had one. Online and telephone purchases usually require a credit card, so it might not be a good idea to destroy every one that you have.

If you have a debit card this problem is solved. This is the ideal solution because the debit card automatically deducts the cost of your purchase from your checking account, making it the equivalent of using cash. I much prefer this approach to carrying a regular credit card because it eliminates the risk of incurring additional debt. I recognize, however, that many families in financial difficulty live from month to month and don't always have extra money sitting in their checking account. If you are buying an airline ticket with commissions you've already earned but which won't be received until the fifteenth of next month, you'll need to buy the ticket in advance in order to get a good price. If you have no excess cash in your checking account, the debit card is not an option.

Very few families have only one credit card. Folks that have accumulated an excessive amount of credit-card debt usually have a number of cards with balances owing. Since spending has been a problem, we do want to eliminate this risk by getting rid of most of the cards. I generally recommend selecting one card to keep and destroying the rest. The best one to keep will usually be the one with the lowest available credit line, preferably $500 or $1,000. This card is usually at or near the credit limit so there isn't much additional damage that can be done. You might want a few hundred dollars of available credit for convenience purposes such as the airline ticket mentioned above, but our main objective is to eliminate credit-card spending as a way of life. Your preference will probably be to keep the card with the largest credit line and several thousand dollars of unused credit, but this will not help you change the habit that caused the problems. We want to keep one card for convenience and necessity, but remove the temptation to continue spending inappropriately.

REFLECT

How many credit cards do you currently have? How many have outstanding balances? Do you think this is excessive?

_____

_____

_____

_____

_____

_____

_____

One certain objection to destroying one's credit cards is, "What about emergencies? If I had a lot of cash I wouldn't have all this debt. What if I cut up my credit cards and then my transmission goes out? I'll have a financial emergency and nothing to pay it with." That is correct. The point often lost is that, even if you had a credit card, you still wouldn't have any money to pay for the emergency. Remember that available credit is not cash, and it doesn't belong to you. This is where we learn about God's provision, a lesson that came home to my family after the career change I described in an earlier chapter.

My wife and I had made two significant commitments a couple of years into our walk with Christ: downsizing our lifestyle, and cutting up our stack of credit cards. The credit cards had been a security blanket prior to my coming to faith in Jesus, and I remember well the combination of fear and freedom that I felt when we finally decided to destroy them. I had already changed jobs at that point, which led to a 50 percent reduction in income. The downsizing process was taking much longer than we had hoped due to the real estate recession in 1994, and we had been unable to sell our home. The mortgage payment was much larger than we could afford, and we were desperately praying that God would intervene. The number of ways in which we saw God work, and the number of people through whom He worked, were too numerous to detail in this chapter. I will, however, share one example because it was the day I truly came to understand that it is God who provides for all of my needs.

This event took place just after Lori and I began tithing. She called me at work on a Tuesday to let me know we were essentially out of food and milk. We had been cutting back while downsizing so our groceries budget had been reduced to cover only necessities; there was no longer any excess food in the house. I still remember how I felt when Lori called, because for the first time in my financial life I didn't have an answer. During my years of reckless spending this temporary problem would have been easily resolved by pulling out one of our credit cards. But my stewardship journey had led me to destroy all but one just the month before, and the one we kept was selected because of its low credit limit and lack of available credit.

The sense of liberation I had felt in destroying those credit cards was quickly giving way once again to that feeling of slipping beneath the waves. This day represented the first instance in my married life that I was unable to provide for the needs of my family. I felt a pain in my heart that I have never known, either before or since.

All we could do is pray. Lori was clearly afraid, and I couldn't do anything to help. Then it happened. Later that morning the doorbell rang and some ladies from church were standing at the door. They explained to Lori that both car trunks were full of groceries for our family. Part of their personal ministry was helping to provide food and clothing for families in need, and God had laid our family on their hearts this particular day. I arrived home that afternoon to God's blessed provision: more than enough food to last us until payday.

I must state that not a single person, save for me and Lori, had any idea of our financial condition. God Himself, through the power of His indwelling Spirit, laid His instruction on the hearts of these precious ladies. They must have wondered as they drove up to this 3,000+ square foot, four-bedroom colonial house with a beautiful built-in swimming pool, whether God had been mistaken. The look of relief, wonder, and gratitude in my wife's eyes quickly confirmed that God, indeed, had led them there.

This is God's way of providing for His children who seek to be faithful and obedient. If we are committed to walking down this road of biblical stewardship, we can trust in God's provision rather than continuing to trust in our credit cards.

REFLECT

Describe an experience in which you have seen God intimately and personally intervene, either in your own circumstances or in those of someone you know.

_____

_____

_____

_____

_____

_____

All of the resources in the world are at God's disposal, and He lovingly makes them available to provide for the needs of His children. Of course, if we insist on violating God's principles of money management we have chosen to go our own way and shouldn't expect God to intervene. But if we are faithfully employing God's Word in the management of our finances, we can trust that He has a solution for the financial emergencies that will inevitably arise. And God's solutions do not involve credit cards.

To summarize, the second step in the process of eliminating your debts is to destroy all credit cards except for one. The one that you keep should either be a debit card or the credit card that has the lowest possible credit line. If you should receive a replacement card in the mail, cut it up as well. If you get a notice of a credit-line increase, call the company and decline it. In order for the wound to heal we must first stop the bleeding. Eliminating the credit cards will eliminate the possibility of going further into debt while we're trying to extricate ourselves from it.

COMMIT

If you have struggled with excessive credit-card debt, resolve to destroy all of your credit cards except one. Commit this matter to the Lord in prayer.

3. LIQUIDATE UNNECESSARY ITEMS. We have identified the problem with consumer debt and resolved to free ourselves from the bondage associated with an excessive debt load. We have repented of the sins that we are aware of which have led to this condition, perhaps a lack of contentment or an unhealthy desire for material possessions. We have started to seek God's guidance and intervention, asking Him to bless our efforts to eliminate the debt and to protect us from falling back into the same patterns that caused it. Finally, we have committed to stop using credit cards for anything other than convenience, purchasing with a credit card only those things that we could otherwise pay cash for within the next thirty days. This commitment was confirmed by destroying all of our credit cards except for one, preferably a debit card or else a credit card with a very low limit and little, if any, available credit.

Now what? The next step will actually be fun, although some sacrifice might also be involved. Make a list of everything you own that has value. Some of us could make such a list off the top of our head, but most people will have to go through every room in the house to develop an accurate inventory. For those to whom this applies, be sure to include the attic and garage in your search, along with any rented storage space or boxes stored with parents or friends. It is extremely important that every material possession of value be included in this list.

APPLY

To help you get started with the liquidation process, list below at least four items in your home that you rarely use and which might have value to someone else.

1. _____
2. _____
3. _____
4. _____

Then start praying. Ask God to give you wisdom to help you determine which things ought to be sold. The money received, of course, will be used to reduce your debt. Few things are more encouraging in the beginning of this process than making a lump-sum payment on your outstanding balance. Most of us have accumulated things over the years that we no longer use. Furniture, tools, books, and sports memorabilia; car seats, changing tables, and high chairs; nearly new clothes that never fit quite right; many of the things we no longer use will have some value to others. Some of these items can be sold at a garage sale, and the larger items might need to be advertised in the local paper. Some will be extremely easy to part with and others very difficult. Spend time in prayer asking God to help you to release some of the things that can bring good value but are hard to relinquish.

The hardest thing I ever had to give up to reduce debt was my pool table. This was something I had wanted for years and which gave me great pleasure when I finally got it. The problem was, like so many other things I had, this purchase was charged to one of many credit cards because I didn't have any money when I decided to buy it. Two years later I was still making the minimum monthly payments, having not reduced the original debt by any noticeable amount. As my wife and I made the decision to downsize our lifestyle, I knew the pool table had to go. I envisioned the buyer having to peel me off the cherry-wood leg as he carried it out the door. I really didn't want to let go, but I knew it was the right thing to do. I got a fair price, the buyer got a meticulously kept, nearly new table for much less than he would have paid in a store, and I was able to use that money to reduce debt.

REFLECT

Share an example of a hard-to-relinquish item that you would be willing to sell in order to reduce your credit-card debt.

As you go through this liquidation process, remember that the amount of money you receive is less important than the process itself. You might not think it is worthwhile to have a garage sale to net $45, but it is worth it because you are demonstrating your commitment to getting out of debt. All money that goes immediately toward debt repayment is significant, regardless of the amount. This is a journey, and the first steps are very important. As I mentioned in an earlier chapter, we need to do everything that we can possibly do, and then trust God to do the part that we can't.

If you can't find anything of value to sell, don't be discouraged. Most of us have been at that place in life where the only way we could downsize was to pay someone else to cart our junk away! Not all of us have things that can be sold, but we'll never know until we go through all of our possessions and make a list. Once that is accomplished, sell whatever you can and use all of the money to reduce your credit-card debt.

COMMIT

If you have credit-card debt that needs to be eliminated, spend a few moments in prayer asking God to make you aware of all items that can and should be sold.

4. REDUCE EXPENSES. One of the key reasons for keeping a monthly budget is to control and account for our monthly spending. When our primary financial objective is debt reduction, we need to scrutinize the budget and make cuts wherever we can. Review every expense to determine whether it can be reasonably reduced in order to free additional cash to apply to your credit-card debt. Some small savings can often be gleaned from our fixed expenses without too much pain. For example, clipping coupons will reduce your grocery bill, as will shopping once or twice each month rather than weekly. The biggest challenge with grocery shopping is impulse buying. Reducing the number of trips to the supermarket will almost certainly reduce overall monthly spending. Similarly, planning our shopping will help to control expenses, and coupon clipping leads to more effective planning. If you want to try and save money on this part of your budget but feel like you haven't been a very wise shopper, ask around your church or neighborhood to see if you can find someone to help you get organized in this area. There are many people who have perfected the art of grocery shopping, and they are often more than willing to share what they have learned.

REFLECT

How many trips do you or your spouse make to the grocery store in a typical week? What is the usual method of payment? How does this impact your impulse buying?

_____

_____

_____

Other fixed expenses that can be easily reduced include the cable TV and telephone bills. Most basic cable TV packages cost $35-40 per month and that usually appears to be the least expensive option. Most carriers, however, have a limited cable option at a much lower rate. They don't advertise it and you might have to call to cancel your cable service in order to find out about it, but the limited package retails for around $10 per month. I've had this package for years and the only thing we're really giving up as far as I can tell are the movie channels. As for the telephone bill, reductions here simply require minimizing the use of long-distance calling. This has been made much easier due to the increasing use of e-mail and instant messaging. Changing your communication habits could cut the phone bill in half.

After you've identified the fixed expenses that can be cut, review your insurance costs. Taking the time to shop around could reduce your premiums for life, auto, and homeowner's insurance. If you have a whole life policy that has become difficult to afford, consider replacing it with term insurance. This strategy is not right for everyone, so talk to a trusted insurance agent or financial advisor before making the switch. I've seen many cases where folks increased their total coverage and dramatically reduced the cost by changing to a policy more appropriate for their current needs.

Another area that could result in a significant cost reduction is eliminating your mortgage insurance. Mortgage lenders will require mortgage insurance when we have less than 20 percent equity in our home. Because the monthly premium is included in our mortgage payment, we tend to forget about it. Many homeowners continue paying for this coverage for years after they could have eliminated it. If you are still paying for mortgage insurance but your equity exceeds 20 percent of the value of your home, call your lender and ask about terminating this coverage. If there is some question about the value of your home it might be necessary to pay for an appraisal. Even so, that cost pales in comparison to years of unnecessary premium payments.

APPLY

If you have a mortgage, are you currently paying mortgage insurance? _____
What is the monthly cost? _____
Do you have more than 20% equity in your home? _____

Now consider your discretionary spending. This is where the bulk of the savings can occur. Are you buying lunch every day at work? It is much less expensive to bring a lunch from home. Are you eating dinner out once a week? Cut back to once or twice a month. Do you have any regular hobbies such as golf or tennis lessons, or do you indulge in visits to the tanning salon? Consider reducing or eliminating these for a short period of time or until the debt is repaid. Remember that prayer is a key component in this process.

Keep in mind that the flesh will not want to eliminate anything; we prefer to deal with stress by spending more, not less. Pray fervently for God's strength and direction. If there is an area that is necessary to cut but you feel yourself resisting, God will change your heart and enable you to do the right thing. Remember that most of these reductions are temporary, so stay focused on the desired outcome rather than dwelling on what you're giving up.

APPLY

List below several specific spending areas in your budget than can be reduced.

1. _____

2. _____

3. _____

4. _____

5. INCREASE YOUR INCOME. This step is a very important part of the debt-reduction strategy, although it might not be possible for everyone. If you are an hourly or part-time employee, ask about increasing your hours or working overtime. If your employer balks, consider getting a second part-time job or a temporary job. If you are a stay-at-home mom, consider caring for another child in order to generate additional income. If you are very artistic and great with crafts, see if a local craft shop will sell your wares. Pet and plant sitting is becoming popular; distribute fliers in your neighborhood and see if anyone is interested. Most dog owners, for example, would much prefer to have their pet cared for in their home when they travel rather than leaving it in a kennel. This is a great opportunity to earn some additional income.

DISCOVER

Write out Proverbs 12:11.

_____

_____

_____

Unlike budget cuts, which have some natural limitations, your ability to earn additional income is limited only by your willingness to work and the number of hours in a day. There was a time in my life that I needed to earn a certain sum of money within three months in order to achieve a particular goal. I worked two full-time jobs for those three months. I worked the graveyard shift stocking shelves in a supermarket, followed by the day shift in a fast food restaurant. I could never have maintained this pace for a long period of time, but it was worth it for a few months in order to achieve the goal.

God's primary means of supplying our needs is through work. Two examples from the Bible come to mind. The first is found in 2 Kings 4:1-7, in which the prophet Elisha was ministering to a widow. Her creditors were about to take her two sons as slaves because she had no money with which to pay her debts. Elisha asked her, *"Tell me, what do you have in your house?"* (This is not unlike the inventory of your possessions that I've asked you to take.) The widow lamented that she had *"nothing at all, except a little oil."* Elisha instructed her to go to her neighbors and collect as many jars as she could, and then God multiplied her oil to an amount sufficient to fill every jar. When all the jars were filled, the oil stopped flowing. The widow then received her instructions: *"Go, sell the oil and pay your debts. You and your sons can live on what is left"* (verse 7).

I used to wonder why, since God was going to perform a miracle anyway, He didn't just make some money appear. It seemed like it wouldn't have been any more work on His part and the end result would have been the same. But that is not how God usually operates. Work is important to God, and laziness is continually condemned in Scripture.

DISCOVER

Read Proverbs 6:9-10 and 10:4. What are some of the words used to describe the result of laziness?

_____

_____

_____

_____

_____

Even though God directly intervened to help this poor widow, He chose to put her in a position to solve the problem rather then solving it for her. She had to work by collecting the jars and then selling the oil. The resulting income was to be used to pay off her debts and provide for her family.

We see a similar approach in Matthew 17:24-27, when Jesus and the disciples entered Capernaum. Peter was asked by the collectors of the two-drachma temple tax, *"Doesn't your teacher pay the temple tax?"* (verse 24). Peter replied that Jesus did indeed pay the tax, and then he conferred with Jesus, who instructed him to *"go to the lake and throw out your line. Take the first fish you catch; open its mouth and you will find a four-drachma coin. Take it and give it to them for my tax and yours"* (verse 27).

What was Peter's profession? He was a fisherman by trade. It seems a bit strange that, having just arrived in a new town to preach about the kingdom of God, Jesus sends Peter out on a fishing expedition. Jesus, who healed the sick and raised the dead, was going to make a coin appear in the mouth of the first fish Peter caught. Why not just make the coin appear in Peter's sandal or some other more convenient place? Jesus could have provided this money through any means that He chose, but His choice was to have Peter get it through his work. If it had been me instead of Peter, Jesus would probably have done it differently; I couldn't catch a fish if my life depended on it. Maybe Jesus' instruction to me would have been, "Go to the church on the corner and offer to teach a workshop on stewardship. The amount they pay you will be exactly the amount needed to pay my tax and yours."

DISCOVER

Read 2 Thessalonians 3:10. State in your own words the basic principle taught in this passage.

_____

_____

Increasing income is an important part of the debt reduction process. For those of us who are physically able, doing additional work is the most logical step. It is God who has given us the ability to earn money through working (see Deuteronomy 8:18), and work is the most common way in which He provides for the needs of His people.

6. RESTRUCTURE, CONSOLIDATE, AND PAY DOWN. The final part of the process involves strategically paying down each credit card and, at times, restructuring your debt in order to repay it more quickly with less expense. Allow me to speak a word of caution, however, about debt restructuring. Don't take this step until you have made a firm commitment to getting out of debt. Otherwise, restructuring will only lead you further into debt.

The term *restructuring* refers to changing the form or terms of your debt. An example would be taking out a home equity loan, which usually has a lower interest rate than credit cards and the interest is tax deductible, and using the loan proceeds to pay off credit-card debt. Economically, this is an excellent decision. Practically, however, it is comparable to handling a loaded gun. The reason we have credit-card debt in the first place is because we lack spending discipline and constantly purchase things we can't afford. In such cases, the most dangerous thing we can be given is a handful of credit cards that are paid off. It looks like free money.

REFLECT

If this applies to you or someone you know, share an example in which the restructuring of debt eventually led to an even larger amount of consumer debt.

_____

_____

_____

_____

_____

Once we're absolutely committed to eliminating all of our debt, however, this kind of restructuring can be very profitable. Another method involves replacing higher-interest-rate credit cards with those with lower rates. If you have credit cards with local department or electronics stores, the interest rates might be higher than you could get on a new major credit card. Transferring a $3,000 balance from a 19.99 percent rate to an 11.99 percent rate will reduce your monthly interest expense by $20. If you continued making the same total payment as before, that full $20 would go to principal repayment.

Many credit-card companies are now offering cards with a zero-percent rate on transferred balances for the first year. This means that you would have the first twelve months with every dollar going directly to principal. Be careful though; many of these companies will charge an up-front balance transfer fee of several percentage points. Make sure you read the fine print of any such offer. Restructuring your credit-card debt can be a very useful strategy. Just make sure you immediately destroy a card after you transfer the balance, if you've not already done so.

When trying to determine the most effective order in which to repay the credit cards, start by writing out a list of all accounts that currently have an outstanding balance. List the creditor, amount owed, total credit line, interest rate, and minimum monthly payment. As you look at the list you will probably see a few candidates for consolidation. Suppose you have a major credit card at 9.99 percent with a $600 balance, a $1,000 credit limit, and a minimum payment of $20. You also have a department store card at 21.99 percent with a $400 balance and a payment of $10 per month. It would be wise to call the major credit-card company and ask if you can transfer the balance of the other card while maintaining the same rate of 9.99 percent. Then continue paying the same $30 per month but, because it all goes to the one card and that interest rate is lower, much more of your payment goes to principal reduction. Be on the watch for these types of opportunities.

APPLY

To help you get started with restructuring your consumer debt, please answer the following questions.

1. Which of your debts currently has the highest interest rate? What is the rate?

_____

_____

2. Which of your debts has the highest outstanding balance? Write the amount.

_____

_____

3. Which of your debts has the lowest outstanding balance? Write the amount.

_____

_____

4. Which of your debts has the highest monthly payment? How much is it?

_____

_____

The most effective way to repay credit-card debt is to start by accelerating the account with the highest interest rate first. Once that is paid off, move to the next highest interest rate, combining the normal monthly payment on that card with the amount that you had been paying on the one that is now paid off. This is the most common approach, and I would suggest only one modification. The more monthly payments we can get rid of, the more money we have available each month to reduce principal on another credit card. If you have several smaller accounts (i.e., cards with $600, $400, and $350 balances) and relatively low interest rates, but the minimum payment is $25 on each, it might make sense to repay these first even though you have other cards at higher rates. Why? Because eliminating these will free $75 per month, all of which can then be applied directly to the principal of the next card you start working on. You will also feel greatly encouraged by getting rid of three of the debts so quickly, which will provide great motivation for continuing the process.

The Next Step

We've covered a great deal of ground in this chapter, and you might need to read this material again at some point in order to absorb all of the information. I believe that the best way to remember what we learn is to apply the information as soon as possible after learning it. To that end, the next chapter presents a case study of a family that has found themselves in financial disarray. We will walk together through the counseling process, giving you the opportunity to apply what you have learned in this study. You will see how these principles are applied to a real family with the same kinds of financial problems that many of us are experiencing today. Join me in guiding this family through the five steps to financial freedom: giving, setting goals, saving, budgeting, and debt reduction.

STUDY QUESTIONS

1. List the six steps described in this chapter that you can take to eliminate debt.

_____

_____

_____

_____

_____

_____

2. Why is prayer such an important part of the debt-elimination process?

_____

_____

_____

3. How can destroying your credit cards open the door to God's provision when a financial emergency arises?

_____

_____

_____

4. What is the most common way in which God provides income to meet our material needs?

_____

_____

_____

5. What potential danger can arise when we consolidate all of our credit-card debts into one loan?

_____

_____

_____

Implementation

-14-
APPLICATION
PART 1

"His master replied, 'You wicked, lazy servant!...Take the talent from him and give it to the one who has the ten talents.'"

—The Parable of the Talents, Matthew 25:26a,28

"Well done, good and faithful servant! You have been faithful with a few things; I will put you in charge of many things. Come and share your master's happiness!"

—The Parable of the Talents, Matthew 25:21

When the time comes for us to stand before the Lord to give an account for our management of the resources He has entrusted to us, which of these two responses do you expect to hear? If you have been a "good and faithful servant," it is my prayer that you will devote some of your time to helping others do likewise. If, on the other hand, you are concerned that you might be the target of the Master's rebuke, I want to encourage you that there is still time to change. Like the father of the Prodigal Son, your Father in heaven will lovingly receive you back, providing the guidance and resources that you need to become a faithful steward. If you start managing money His way, you will most certainly succeed, to the praise of His glory.

I have two very specific purposes for the next three chapters. For those who have been blessed to learn these principles early in life and who already consistently implement them, my desire is that you might be moved to counsel those around you who are struggling financially. Even if you have little or no counseling experience, I'm hopeful that this book might provide a structure for guiding someone to improved financial health. My second objective is that those who are struggling with money management will use these principles in order to turn their own financial lives around.

People are usually more objective when reviewing someone else's circumstances than they are with their own, so we'll use a case study as practice for implementing these principles in our own lives. We'll look at some of the financial challenges faced by a typical family and walk them, step by step, through the process of implementing the five steps to financial freedom.

It is my hope that these exercises will help illuminate these principles and make it easier for you to apply them in your own life.

DISCOVER

Write out John 13:17 and James 1:22. Take a moment and pray that the Lord will make these verses real in your life.

John 13:17

_____

_____

_____

James 1:22

_____

_____

_____

Case Study

Mike and Mary Jones live with their three children in a middle-class suburban neighborhood. Although they have never kept a written budget, they always felt they were doing well financially because they've been able to pay the bills each month and usually put a small amount into their savings account. More recently, however, they have been experiencing greater levels of stress because their monthly bills seem to be higher than their income. They had never worried about credit-card use before because they were always able to make the payments, but now they can only make the minimum payments and therefore are not reducing the principal amount of their debt. They've also been forced to withdraw from their savings for the past few months just to pay the regular bills.

Although Mike and Mary have always gotten along well, discussions about money in the past several months have resulted in arguments. As a result, even though they realize there are financial problems under the surface, they now avoid discussing them. Mary pays the bills each month and wants Mike to get involved so he can better see that their spending is not under control. Mike wants Mary to return to full-time employment, at least until the income shortfall is resolved. Mary's dream has always been to be a stay-at-home mom, but she and Mike never discuss long-term objectives because setting goals together has never been a priority.

Mike's primary hobbies are watching sports on cable TV and occasionally taking motorcycle trips with his friends. Mary has recently taken up weekly tennis lessons. As their relationship has become more strained, their church attendance has been irregular. They are both feeling some level of guilt because their tight budget has led them to stop tithing, and Mike is uncomfortable around their friends because he doesn't want them to know about his financial struggles. As a result, he has started working late on Tuesday nights to avoid attending their small group Bible study.

When it comes time to pay the bills each month there is great tension in the house, which the kids have started to notice. The result is usually that Mike and Mary withdraw into their respective hobbies, each quietly blaming the other for the financial disarray in which they find themselves.

Spiritual and Financial Issues

Before we start working through the five steps, I think it is important to identify the specific issues with which Mike and Mary are grappling. Not only do the finances need to be repaired, but the communication also needs to be restored. When counseling a couple rather than an individual, we must look at different sets of priorities, as well as try to assess the sin and selfishness that are exacerbating the problems in the relationship. As we work together through this case, it might become necessary to refer back to the Joneses' specific circumstances in order to understand the best counsel to give. Take a minute now to review the case study, completing the worksheet below as you do so. In the space provided, make a note of each specific issue that needs to be dealt with and whether that issue is primarily spiritual or financial in nature.

After completing this exercise, compare your list to the one on the page that follows to see if you missed any significant issues.

—Mike and Mary Jones: Counseling Issues—

Financial Issues

1. _____
2. _____
3. _____
4. _____
5. _____

Spiritual Issues

1. _____
2. _____
3. _____
4. _____
5. _____
6. _____

The reason this exercise is important is that financial counsel should always be tailored to the particular individuals and their needs. Some of the recommendations we'll make will hold true for everyone, but others will be case specific. A great example of this is in the area of hobbies. We might deal with this issue differently with Mike and Mary — whose hobbies are not only expensive, but also keeping them apart — than we would with another couple whose only hobby is going camping together. At the same time, we're interested in providing spiritual counsel that will help Mike and Mary grow in their faith. That is why we must assess the spiritual as well as the financial issues.

Note that in the first counseling session I will purposely avoid providing any answers. My job is to listen intently, take good notes, and avoid judging anyone's motives or decision-making skills. I want to go deeper than just understanding the numbers; I want to know where this couple is, both personally and spiritually. Sometimes personal and relational challenges lead to spending problems, and sometimes it is the other way around. I hope to determine how things got to this point and look for areas of agreement that can be used as a foundation for my counsel.

—Mike and Mary Jones: Counseling Issues—

Financial Issues

1. No written budget
2. Spending more than they earn; negative monthly cash flow
3. Depleting, rather than adding to, savings
4. Lack of financial goals
5. High level of debt relative to income; minimum credit-card payments not reducing loan balances

Spiritual Issues

1. Not tithing
2. Distance in the relationship; hobbies are separate rather than together
3. Refusal to accept responsibility for financial condition
4. Negative impact on children
5. Isolation from church and friends
6. Avoidance of problem rather than seeking counsel

After we've identified some of the important issues in need of attention, and have prayed fervently for God's wisdom and intervention, we are ready to begin providing counsel.

As we go forward, I will use the same format for each of the five steps in order to simplify the process: Mike's perspective, Mary's perspective, their compromise, and key biblical principles that apply. Where appropriate, I will leave space for you to write your own solutions before I share the suggestions I would make to this couple.

Step 1: Giving

Let me mention at the outset that my approach here differs from many Christian counselors. I am absolutely convinced that giving is foundational to the process of implementing biblical financial principles and repairing financial damage. I believe God when He says that if we fail to give, we are robbing Him, and if we test Him in this, He will pour out His blessings upon us (Malachi 3:8-10). As mentioned in a previous chapter, these blessings are not always or only financial, but God promises to bless our obedient giving, and this must be the starting point for change. Our faith is strengthened when we agree to give, especially when money is tight. We must be absolutely persuaded that everything belongs to God and that giving back some portion of what He has entrusted to us is nonnegotiable. Keep in mind, however, that we aren't giving to get something from God. We've already received from God the very income that we are giving back to His work. Our primary motivation is obedience. If we are trusting God to meet all of our needs and we are faithfully obeying His call to give generously, we can pray expectantly for His help in working through our difficult circumstances.

REFLECT

How did you respond to my thoughts on giving? Do you think it is reasonable to begin with encouraging some level of giving? Or do you believe it is more important to try and solve the other problems first, such as the lack of savings or negative cash flow?

_____

_____

_____

_____

_____

In our first counseling session, we begin by discussing the concept of tithing. Assessing where both persons are in regard to this matter will determine the specific counsel I will give. My ultimate objective, for their own benefit, is to encourage them to tithe as soon as possible. I recognize, however, that I am not the Holy Spirit, and

He alone can bring about this conviction. My part is to faithfully share God's teaching on the subject and then encourage them to implement this instruction. Where there is resistance, I remain loving and patient, consistently praying that God will strengthen their faith and lead them to embrace His Word. Following is a summary of both Mike and Mary's perspective on the issue of giving.

—Mike's Perspective—

Mike wouldn't mind tithing if they were in better shape financially. "If God wants us to give more, can't He give us more income to make it possible?" he asks. Because this seems to be a touchy subject for Mike, he might have some underlying guilt over their having stopped giving when the budget got tight. He's willing to take a small "step of faith" by starting to give, but 10 percent at this point just seems unrealistic.

—Mary's Perspective—

Mary believes that tithing is the responsibility of all Christians. Mary has tithed on all of her income since she was a child, and this is the first time in her life that she has not been doing so. She didn't agree with the decision to stop tithing, and she would like to start again, even if it means making sacrifices in other areas.

APPLY

Now that you understand this couple's different perspectives on this important issue, use the space below to write out the counsel you would provide concerning their giving.

_____

_____

_____

_____

_____

_____

_____

—Compromise Decision—

After some discussion and prayer, Mike agreed that they would start giving 5 percent of their gross income for the next six months. During that time they will pray daily that God will lead them to a resolution of their current financial problems. If after six months they see some relief from the financial strain they've been experiencing, Mike will agree to set a time frame within which they will begin giving a full tithe.

—Key Biblical Principles—

"Will a man rob God? Yet you rob me. But you ask, 'How do we rob you?' In tithes and offerings. You are under a curse – the whole nation of you – because you are robbing me. Bring the whole tithe into the storehouse, that there may be food in my house. Test me in this," says the LORD Almighty, "and see if I will not throw open the floodgates of heaven and pour out so much blessing that you will not have room enough for it."

—Malachi 3:8-10

Now about the collection for God's people: Do what I told the Galatian churches to do. On the first day of every week, each one of you should set aside a sum of money in keeping with his income, saving it up, so that when I come no collections will have to be made.

—1 Corinthians 16:1-2

Remember this: Whoever sows sparingly will also reap sparingly, and whoever sows generously will also reap generously. Each man should give what he has decided in his heart to give, not reluctantly or under compulsion, for God loves a cheerful giver.

—2 Corinthians 9:6-7

Step 2: Goals

One of the issues we've identified for Mike and Mary is a lack of specific financial goals. This is not unusual; most individuals and couples have never given much thought to setting long-term financial goals. We tend to be naturally shortsighted with regard to financial matters, rarely thinking beyond the next six months.

When working with couples, it is important to get input from both the husband and the wife. This is usually a great experience for both because each is able to talk about their dreams, knowing that their spouse is listening. It invariably occurs that each person will share one or two strong desires of which the other person wasn't even aware. Sometimes this lack of awareness is because a particular goal has never been mentioned, and sometimes it is because the other person wasn't listening. Whether you are counseling an individual or a couple, encourage each person to be willing to dream. It is our goals that generally drive our behavior, and working through this process will help to bring about whatever behavioral change is needed.

One of the key points that arises during the discussion on goals with the Joneses was just how important it is to Mary to be a stay-at-home mom. Mike could remember this being mentioned in passing, but he had no idea of the significance of this goal for Mary. Their discussion helps Mary to understand the tremendous internal struggle Mike has been experiencing by feeling he is unable to provide for his family. They both realize that blaming each other for the problems is counterproductive, and they have committed to improving their communication and partnership, remembering that they are on the same team.

—Mike's Goals—

1. A positive monthly cash flow
2. To add some amount to savings each month
3. A firm plan to get out of debt
4. Improvement of the marriage through improved communication and the elimination of financial stress

—Mary's Goals—

1. To be a stay-at-home mom
2. Elimination of debt
3. To tithe consistently and give freewill offerings when able
4. More quality time together with freedom from the constant financial stress

APPLY

Now that we've identified the most significant goals for Mike and Mary, what counsel would you give for prioritizing these goals? Would you suggest moving some of the goals to the "back burner" because they don't seem feasible, or would you encourage them to hold fast to all of the goals? Do you see any conflict between their goals?

_____

_____

_____

_____

_____

—Compromise Decision—

Mike and Mary realized quickly that no compromise is necessary because for the most part, they share the same basic goals. Mike admits that the thought of losing Mary's income concerns him, but he is willing to do whatever he can to help make her dream a reality. They both found it very helpful to have this discussion, and they are each just as committed to the other's goals as they are to their own.

—Key Biblical Principles—

I will instruct you and teach you in the way you should go; I will counsel you and watch over you.

—Psalm 32:8

Forget the former things; do not dwell on the past. See, I am doing a new thing! Now it springs up; do you not perceive it? I am making a way in the desert and streams in the wasteland.

—Isaiah 43:18-19

The plans of the diligent lead to profit as surely as haste leads to poverty.

—Proverbs 21:5

Commit to the LORD whatever you do, and your plans will succeed.

—Proverbs 16:3

Step 3: Saving

Even if saving hadn't been one of Mike's top goals, I would have encouraged the Joneses to make this commitment. Saving is an important part of money management and especially when there is an increasing amount of consumer debt, saving makes it possible to start paying cash for financial emergencies rather than using a credit card. The challenge is determining the appropriate amount to save in view of the lack of excess cash flow. It is apparent from our discussion that saving is much more important to Mike at the present time than it is to Mary. Still, it shouldn't be too difficult to reach a compromise on which both can agree.

—Mike's Perspective—

Mike realizes that the discipline of saving is more important than the actual amount saved. He agrees that if they don't "pay themselves first," they probably won't save at all. Although they haven't worked on their budget yet, Mike is intent on saving whatever they can, and he is committed to transferring this amount directly into their savings account before paying their other bills.

—Mary's Perspective—

Mary thinks it is more important to get out of debt before they start worrying about their savings account. She is pleased, however, that Mike is taking such an interest in their finances and in resolving the challenges they face. Mary trusts Mike's judgment and, since he went along with her desires on the giving issue, she is willing to seriously discuss setting a monthly savings goal.

APPLY

Write in the following spaces the specific counsel you would give Mike and Mary in the area of saving. Should they even attempt to do so at this point? Or should they use any excess cash flow that can be created to pay down their debt? Is it realistic to save when cash flow is so tight?

_____

_____

_____

_____

_____

At this point you might be wondering why we are addressing the areas of giving and saving before we've even looked at the budget. The one thing we know for certain is that Mike and Mary have a negative monthly cash flow. "Where," you might be inclined to ask, "will the money come from to give or to save?" That is a reasonable question; let me propose a reasonable answer.

The five steps to financial freedom have been listed in this particular order by design. I noted in a previous chapter that all of the five "spending" areas prescribed in the Scriptures (giving, taxes, saving, living expenses, and debt repayment) are of equal importance and we are called to be faithful in all of them. However, the amount spent on lifestyle must be prudent and reasonable based on our income level and the amounts allocated to the other four areas. Therefore, it is important to arrive at the amounts to be committed to these other areas before determining the lifestyle that we can prudently afford.

If we had begun with the Joneses' budget, we likely would have concluded immediately that their giving and saving were out of the question due to their negative cash flow. Then in addressing any potential budget changes, we would only concentrate on eliminating the cash flow problem. But by starting instead with the giving and saving goals, these objectives become part of the budgeting process and help to define the amount of the Joneses' monthly income that is available for lifestyle.

Most individuals and families that experience financial hardship and excessive debt loads take the opposite approach. A lifestyle is constructed that absorbs all of the after-tax income, leaving no excess for giving or saving. When emergencies arise or the car needs to be replaced, these needs are necessarily funded by additional debt. Suddenly, the cash flow is negative due to increasing debt payments, and the thought of giving or saving seems unrealistic, even impossible.

Since we know that God calls us all to give and to save, as well as pay our taxes and repay our debts, these figures must be determined before we decide what kind of lifestyle we can reasonably afford. The command to provide for the needs of our families is also of utmost importance, but it should deal more with our needs than our wants, especially when money is tight. Usually, when we experience financial hardship and our lifestyle expenses exceed our income, it is often because of the "wants" that we bought but couldn't afford.

Following, then, is the recommendation to which Mike and Mary were able to agree with regard to establishing a regular savings plan.

—Compromise Decision—

They'll follow a similar pattern with saving as with their giving, starting with $100 per month for the first six months. If they see things improving at the end of that period of time, they will increase their saving to $200 per month. Their ultimate objective is to increase to $400 per month, which is slightly more than 10 percent of their combined take-home pay.

—Key Biblical Principles—

If anyone does not provide for his relatives, and especially for his immediate family, he has denied the faith and is worse than an unbeliever.

—1 Timothy 5:8

In the house of the wise are stores of choice food and oil, but a foolish man devours all he has.

—Proverbs 21:20

Go to the ant, you sluggard; consider its ways and be wise! It has no commander, no overseer or ruler, yet it stores its provisions in summer and gathers its food at harvest.

—Proverbs 6:6-8

STUDY QUESTIONS

1. When applying these five steps to a person's circumstances, whether yours or a friend's, which is the first step that should be taken? Why?

_____

_____

_____

2. Why is it important to determine one's goals before developing a budget?

_____

_____

_____

3. Why is it important to save at some level even during difficult financial times?

_____

_____

_____

4. What factors go into determining what kind of lifestyle you can afford?

_____

_____

_____

-15-
APPLICATION
PART 2

"For everyone who has will be given more, and he will have an abundance. Whoever does not have, even what he has will be taken from him."
—Jesus, Matthew 25:29

"Teach me, O LORD, to follow your decrees; then I will keep them to the end."
—King David, Psalm 119:33

It is at this point that the hard work begins. No one enjoys budget cuts, and many of us have never even attempted to keep a budget, so identifying the areas to cut can be quite a challenge. As you can imagine, in the counseling process this becomes one of the most trying and time-consuming steps. I hope to demonstrate, however, that by developing an accurate budget and then considering each expense with the goals and objectives in mind, it is often possible to save a considerable amount each month without eliminating all discretionary expenses.

Let's proceed with helping the Joneses get their current expenses down on paper, and then make some recommendations that will enable them to bring their monthly expenses in line with their income.

Step 4: Budget

There was a noticeable cringe on Mike's face when I asked about the budget. It turned out that Mike had tried to develop a budget twice in the past, but both times he became frustrated with the computer program he was using. It seemed to require hours each month to update the data, and he would have had to save every receipt in order to properly account for their spending. Mike's job was stressful at times, and the last thing he felt like doing when he got home from work was spending another hour or two entering receipts into the budget program. Mike noted that he already had a full-time job and he didn't need another one!

We talked about budgeting from the perspective of creating a simple spending plan. This concept made sense to Mike because he enjoyed planning their family vacations, diligently determining how much they could afford to spend and how that money would be divided among the various activities. We agreed to do away with the computer program and to eliminate the practice of saving receipts. Discretionary spending, which they both acknowledged had become a problem, would now be controlled by using the envelope system. Mike actually liked the idea of deciding in advance how much of their income would be allocated to each expense area. I assured him that it would only take thirty to sixty minutes each month to set up the written budget and that the overspending would end immediately.

We started with a blank budget worksheet, the Joneses' checkbook, and their bills from the past several months. We made a list of their average monthly expenses as compared with their net income. Note that at this point we will only be working on the living expenses; in the next section we'll look at restructuring the debt.

—Mike and Mary Joneses' Monthly Budget—

CATEGORY	AMOUNT	RATE/NOTES
Mortgage	$1,160	8.50% (30-year; 26 years left) (including taxes and insurance)
Home Equity Loan	110	10.50% (15-year; 9 years left)
Car Loan #1	225	11.00% (5-year; 3 years left)
Car Loan #2	265	11.25% (3-year; 1 year left)
Master Card	95	15.90%
Visa	76	16.90%
Discover	60	17.75%
JC Penney Card	25	17.90%
Sears Card	50	18.90%
Giving	40	

CATEGORY	AMOUNT	RATE/NOTES
Saving	$0	
Food	400	
Gas and Electric	190	
Telephone	95	
Cell Phone	75	
Life Insurance	220	Whole life - $300K
Auto Insurance	115	
Motorcycle Insurance	20	
Gas and Oil	120	
Cable TV	60	
Dining Out	160	Once a week
Gym Membership	30	
Lunches Out (Mike)	100	
Tennis Lessons (Mary)	120	
Babysitting	110	
Total Monthly Expenses:	**$3,921**	
Mike's Net Income	2,925	After taxes, insurance
Mary's Net Income	740	After taxes
Total Monthly Income:	**$3,665**	
Margin	($256)	

As you can see, there is a problem. The process of putting the budget in writing has confirmed what Mike suspected all along: They have a negative monthly cash flow. By spending $256 more than they earn each month, their savings account is being depleted and their credit-card use is increasing. In order to solve any problem, however, we must first identify it. Once Mike and Mary got over the initial shock of seeing their budget in black and white, it was relatively easy for them to agree that immediate and dramatic action was required in order to reverse the problem.

In addition, you may recall that we seem to have made the problem worse in the first three steps. The Joneses have made a commitment to giving 5 percent of their gross income, or $200 a month, and to saving at least $100 a month. These two decisions may have made the immediate negative cash flow problem worse, but there are steps they can take to improve the situation.

APPLY

Take a few minutes and review the Joneses' living expenses, making a note of which specific items you would advise them to cut and what the revised figure should be. As you do, keep in mind the financial and spiritual issues that we discussed in the previous chapter. Make sure that you give a reason for every suggested cut, and that your reason addresses one or more specific issues that we want to help improve.

EXPENSE	CURRENT	REVISED
Giving	$40	$200
Saving	0	100
Food	400	_____
Gas and Electric	190	_____
Telephone	95	_____
Cell Phone	75	_____
Life Insurance	220	_____
Auto Insurance	115	_____
Motorcycle Insurance	20	_____
Gas and Oil	120	_____
Cable TV	60	_____
Dining Out	160	_____
Gym Membership	30	_____
Lunches Out (Mike)	100	_____
Tennis Lessons (Mary)	120	_____
Babysitting	110	_____

In the space below please list every specific revision you are recommending and note your reason for each. As already noted, you will find it helpful to refer back to the list of spiritual and financial issues we've identified that we are

endeavoring to resolve in this process. List only the expense areas for which you recommended a revision.

EXPENSE	REASON FOR RECOMMENDATION
_____	_____
_____	_____
_____	_____
_____	_____
_____	_____
_____	_____
_____	_____
_____	_____
_____	_____
_____	_____
_____	_____
_____	_____

Now compare your recommendations to the following revised budget, which reflects the actual changes the Joneses agreed to make in this first round of budget cuts. Any changes made and their accompanying notes are in italics for easy identification. The detailed rationale for these revisions will follow.

—Mike and Mary Joneses' Revised Budget—

CATEGORY	REVISED AMOUNT	EXPLANATION
Giving	$200	*Increased per step 1*
Saving	100	*Increased per step 3*
Food	400	
Gas and Electric	175	*Reduced heating/air conditioner use*
Telephone	70	*Reduced long-distance calling*
Cell Phone	30	*Shopped for less expensive plan*
Life Insurance	45	*Converted to $500K term policy*
Auto Insurance	105	*Shopped for better rate*

CATEGORY	REVISED AMOUNT	EXPLANATION
Motorcycle Insurance	$20	
Gas and Oil	120	
Cable TV	30	*Cancelled premium channels*
Dining Out	100	*Reduced to twice a month*
Gym Membership	0	*Eliminated*
Lunches Out (Mike)	20	*Reduced to 2-4 times a month*
Tennis Lessons (Mary)	0	*Eliminated*
Babysitting	40	*Reduced due to previous changes*
Total Monthly Expenses:	**$3,521**	*Reduced by $400 a month*
Mike's Net Income	2,925	After taxes, insurance
Mary's Net Income	740	After taxes
Total Monthly Income:	**$3,665**	
Margin	144	*Improved from ($256)*

The most important thing to note is that, despite the increase in giving and saving, the overall budget was reduced by $400 a month. These changes took the Joneses from a cash flow margin of negative $256 to positive $144 each month. Some of these recommended changes were relatively minor (gas and electric, telephone, cell phone, auto insurance, and cable TV) and self-explanatory. Others were more significant and an explanation might be helpful.

1. LIFE INSURANCE: Mike's whole life policy was too expensive and provided less coverage ($300K death benefit) than he needs. He was able to find a term life policy with a major insurer with a $500K death benefit for $45 per month, saving $175 per month.

2. DINING OUT: Although this was the only activity that Mike and Mary did together or as a family, they both realized that they couldn't afford to go out every week. We agreed that it was important to keep this activity in the budget, especially in view of their joint goal of strengthening their marriage. We reduced the monthly amount from $160 to $100, saving $60 a month.

3. GYM MEMBERSHIP: This was a relatively easy decision because neither of them had been using the membership regularly. They did discuss the importance of getting their exercise and decided to take walks together after dinner several evenings each week. This will help to achieve the goal of spending more time together and also save $30 per month.

4. LUNCHES OUT (MIKE): This was another easy decision. Mike had gotten into the habit of eating fast food every day, which wasn't beneficial for either his health or his wallet. Mary gladly offered to make Mike a lunch every day, and they'll continue to budget $20 a month so that Mike can still go out occasionally. This change saves $80 a month.

5. TENNIS LESSONS: It was interesting to watch Mary process this decision. It turns out that she wasn't terribly interested in tennis, and she acknowledged that her motivation was sinful. She knew their finances were tight, but because she resented Mike's motorcycle trips with his friends, she had decided to do something for herself, even though they couldn't afford it. There was great healing in the relationship as we discussed this issue and concluded that the tennis lessons had to go. Total savings: $120 per month.

6. BABYSITTING: As a necessary consequence of going out less and eliminating the gym membership and tennis lessons, the babysitting expense was automatically reduced. We purposely kept $40 in the budget for this purpose to ensure that Mike and Mary could honor their commitment to go out a couple of times each month.

Some readers may be protesting vehemently at this point: "What about that stupid motorcycle?" Whenever I've conducted this exercise in a workshop, asking the class to identify specific budget reductions, the men will object to Mary's tennis lessons and the women will unanimously reject Mike's motorcycle. Obviously, the motorcycle is an issue for several reasons. One is the cost, not only the insurance ($20/month) but also the unbudgeted cost of Mike's occasional weekend trips with his friends. Another issue is that this is one of the activities that has kept Mike and Mary apart, enabling Mike to isolate himself when the financial pressure became overwhelming. (Someone in the class is usually quick to point out that motorcycles are also unsafe, but I have friends and family members who would argue that point!) But another important consideration, though less obvious, is that the motorcycle represents an asset with some value, which might eventually be sold to reduce debt. There are many reasons to include this in the discussion.

So why didn't this supposedly experienced counselor (me) insist that Mike get rid of the motorcycle? This is where patience and compassion come into play, as well as good listening skills. Mike got his first dirt bike when he was eight years old and his fondest memories with his dad include the many weekend trips they would take together as he was growing up. During his teen years, Mike would spend hours after school working with his dad to either repair or rebuild an old motorcycle. Mike's dad was one of the men that would go on the occasional weekend trips with him, at least until his unexpected death two years ago. Although Mike's son hasn't yet shown any interest in motorcycles, Mike was always hopeful that this hobby might eventually become something they could enjoy together.

As you can see, counseling is not always black and white. We must be sensitive to the history of those we are seeking to help. Remember also that, as noted earlier, I am not the Holy Spirit, and I will not attempt to do His work. The last thing we discussed at the end of this session was Mike's feelings about the motorcycle and his long-term plans for it. The magnitude of this decision became immediately evident, as did Mary's concern about the safety issue. I asked each of them to make one commitment. I asked Mike to commit this matter to intense prayer to see how the Lord might lead him. I asked Mary to agree that, unless Mike felt clearly led by the Lord to give up the motorcycle, it would not be discussed again for at least a year. This couple was making progress and didn't need the burden of having an ongoing disagreement about a major issue. We had to trust God to provide His clear direction, and leave Mike to make this decision for himself.

A great deal of progress has been made to this point, so let me summarize briefly the Joneses' different perspectives as we worked through the budget revisions.

—Mike's Perspective—

Mike realizes that in order to accomplish their goals they will both need to make sacrifices. He has also become concerned that his tendency to withdraw is taking away from valuable family time and contributing to marital stress. Mike is willing to cut back dramatically on the time he spends watching TV, and he is considering at least reducing the regularity of his motorcycle trips if it will help accomplish the immediate goals of relieving financial strain and accelerating debt repayment.

—Mary's Perspective—

Mary feels some guilt over the unnecessary expenses on which she had insisted, particularly the gym membership and tennis lessons. Mary was blessed by the way that Mike handled this part of the discussion, and she was quick to suggest that these expenses be eliminated. She would much prefer having a joint hobby, something they could do together regularly. Mary is willing to do, or give up, whatever is necessary in order to eliminate the monthly financial stress and restore the family relationships.

—Compromise Objectives—

Mike agreed to eliminate the premium cable TV channels while Mary, as noted above, gave up the gym and tennis lessons. They reviewed every budget item and agreed to make the planned cuts in all of the areas listed in the revised budget. They were surprised at how much immediate impact these cuts would make on their monthly cash flow, and they are excited about their progress so far. Mike has agreed to pray about what to do with his motorcycle.

—Key Biblical Principles—

"Suppose one of you wants to build a tower. Will he not first sit down and estimate the cost to see if he has enough money to complete it?"

—Luke 14:28

The prudent see danger and take refuge, but the simple keep going and suffer for it.

—Proverbs 27:12

He who ignores discipline comes to poverty and shame.

—Proverbs 13:18

In his heart a man plans his course, but the LORD determines his steps.

—Proverbs 16:9

STUDY QUESTIONS

1. Why is it important that a budget be in writing?

_____

_____

_____

2. How do a person's goals impact their budget, especially with regard to their discretionary spending?

_____

_____

_____

3. In a counseling situation, why is it important to understand the history of each person you are trying to help?

_____

_____

_____

4. When a person or family is struggling financially, why is there often a reluctance to draft a budget?

_____

_____

_____

5. What keeps those in financial trouble from seeking the counsel they need?

_____

_____

_____

-16-
APPLICATION
PART 3

"The blessing of the LORD brings wealth, and he adds no trouble to it."

—King Solomon, Proverbs 10:22

"Whoever gives heed to instruction prospers, and blessed is he who trusts in the LORD."

—King Solomon, Proverbs 16:20

In the last chapter we were able to achieve some significant monthly savings by recommending certain reductions in the Joneses' living expenses. The next step in this process, which will also have a direct impact on the budget, is restructuring and eliminating their debt. This part of the process may require a bit more creativity than the other steps, but you'll find that, if handled prudently, it can have the greatest immediate impact on reducing monthly outflows.

Step 5: Debt Reduction and Elimination

The first step in dealing with the debt problem is to create a statement of net worth, listing all of the Joneses' assets and liabilities. We have two objectives as we review this information: 1) to identify assets that can be liquidated in order to free funds for debt repayment, and 2) to look for opportunities to restructure some of the higher-interest debt. As we create a pool of funds to be used for debt elimination, we'll have to make decisions as to the order in which these debts should be repaid.

—Mike and Mary Joneses' Statement of Net Worth—

ASSETS		LIABILITIES	
Home	$135,000	Mortgage	$102,000
Checking Account	1,200	Home Equity Loan	7,500
Savings Account	5,600	Master Card	4,700
IRA (Mike)	9,500	Visa	3,800
Stocks, Mutual Funds	13,100	Discover	2,400
Motorcycle	3,600	JC Penney Card	1,900
Cash Value Life Insurance	5,300	Sears Card	1,200
Car 1	12,000	Car Loan 1	6,200
Car 2	7,400	Car Loan 2	2,300
Total Assets	**$192,700**	**Total Liabilities**	**$132,000**

Total Assets:	$192,700
Total Liabilities:	($132,000)
NET WORTH:	$60,700

APPLY

Review carefully the Joneses' net-worth statement and make a list of your recommended changes below. Your advice might include the sale of assets, liquidation of investments, debt repayment, and debt restructuring (i.e., using a new, lower-interest-rate loan to repay a high-interest-rate loan or credit card). Where applicable, list the reason for your recommendation.

ASSETS	CURRENT	REVISED
Home	**$135,000**	_____
Checking Account	**1,200**	_____
Savings Account	**5,600**	_____
IRA (Mike)	**9,500**	_____
Stocks, Mutual Funds	**13,100**	_____
Motorcycle	**3,600**	_____
Cash Value Life Insurance	**5,300**	_____
Car 1	**12,000**	_____
Car 2	**7,400**	_____

LIABILITIES

Mortgage	$102,000	_____
Home Equity Loan	7,500	_____
Master Card	4,700	_____
Visa	3,800	_____
Discover	2,400	_____
JC Penney Card	1,900	_____
Sears Card	1,200	_____
Car Loan 1	6,200	_____
Car Loan 2	2,300	_____

Now list your reasons for the recommendations made above.

ASSET LIQUIDATED/REDUCED	REASON
_____	_____
_____	_____
_____	_____
_____	_____
_____	_____
_____	_____
_____	_____
_____	_____
_____	_____
_____	_____

DEBTS REPAID	REASON
_____	_____
_____	_____
_____	_____
_____	_____
_____	_____
_____	_____
_____	_____
_____	_____
_____	_____

DEBTS RESTRUCTURED   **REASON**

_____   _____

_____   _____

_____   _____

_____   _____

_____   _____

_____   _____

_____   _____

ADDITIONAL NOTES OR SUGGESTIONS

_____

_____

_____

_____

_____

_____

_____

_____

Mike just received a tax refund, which was deposited into the checking account for the time being. Mike and Mary had been accustomed to keeping at least $1,000 in their checking account at all times, to insure partly for small emergencies and partly against bouncing any checks, even if they inadvertently missed recording a transaction or two. In recent months, however, the checking account had been reaching zero before the end of every month, which made them very uncomfortable. We agreed that it was okay to keep some amount in reserve, but $1,000 seemed excessive in view of the more urgent need to eliminate debt. We decided to hold $500 in the checking account, but remove it from the check register so there wouldn't be any temptation to draw on this money for impulse spending. They might still see the check-register balance decline to zero each month, but they would know that they had an emergency reserve in the account, which would protect against bouncing checks. This strategy might seem unnecessary to some people, but the fact is that money in the checkbook usually gets spent. An action as simple as deducting that reserve from the check register will often eliminate the temptation to spend it. This decision will free $700 for debt repayment.

As you can see, the Joneses have some assets to work with, which isn't always the case. (If there are no assets to liquidate you simply move on to the next step of looking for ways to increase income.) Mike and Mary must now decide which assets to liquidate and in what amounts. They have $5,600 left in savings, down from $8,000 just a year ago. They are reluctant to use their savings to repay debt because this account has decreased so much, but I've helped them to see that repaying the debt will allow them to accelerate their saving later. The target amount we agreed to hold in savings is $3,800, roughly the amount of one month's take-home pay for Mike and Mary. As a result, another $1,800 is available to reduce debt.

You might be aware that liquidating an IRA can be very costly because the entire amount withdrawn must be taxed and, if you are under age 59 1/2, there is an additional 10 percent penalty. Some advisors will never counsel anyone to liquidate their retirement assets, regardless of the severity of the debt problems. In certain cases I have been willing to recommend liquidating an IRA account, but those instances are few and far between. The Joneses' financial situation is not yet serious enough for me to consider making this recommendation.

I will suggest, however, that they sell off some of their stocks and mutual fund investments. The interest rates on most of their credit cards are higher than the average expected return on the investments. Even if that were not the case, I would still make this recommendation. It is not a purely economic decision. Proverbs 22:7 rightly states that *the rich rule over the poor, and the borrower is servant to the lender.* Having debt, especially credit-card debt, equates to financial bondage. If you are a slave to debt and God has blessed you with some assets that can be liquidated to reduce that debt, you are on solid biblical ground in making that decision. Don't be concerned about the yield on the liquidated security — worry instead about sleeping at night.

As I reviewed the Joneses' investments, it became obvious that there was virtually no capital appreciation to deal with. The holdings were evenly divided between gains and losses, so we could sell some of these securities without any tax implication. The decision was to reduce the investment portfolio to $3,400, thus freeing $9,700 for debt repayment. Remember also that, in the section on budgeting, we had decided to terminate the whole life policy and replace it with term insurance. This decision made the cash-surrender value of the whole life policy available. Remember that, since this cash value was building on a tax-deferred basis, there would be some ordinary income taxes due on the liquidated amount. The entire amount would not be taxed; only the portion that represents interest earnings on the policy is subject to income taxes. We are estimating that, of the $5,300 cash value, the Joneses will net approximately $4,400 after taxes are paid.

The final decision was by far the most difficult, although you wouldn't have known it by the look on Mike's face. He had decided to sell his motorcycle, and he was actually excited about the decision. He reasoned that strengthening the marriage and family was a priority over his own leisure activity. He also wanted to make some personal sacrifice to get the family back on track financially, and this was his opportunity to demonstrate to Mary that he was committed to the process of getting out of debt. Mike realized that, once they were out of debt, if he missed this hobby or if his son should ever start to develop an interest in motorcycles, they could always consider replacing it at that time. This sale generated $3,600.

Following is a revised net-worth statement for Mike and Mary which shows each liquidation decision and the debts that were repaid as a result. Once again, the revisions are noted in italics for easy identification.

—Mike and Mary Joneses' Revised Statement of Net Worth—

ASSETS		Reduced To:	$ Made Available:
Home	$135,000	$135,000	
Checking Account	1,200	500	$700
Savings Account	5,600	3,800	1,800
IRA (Mike)	9,500	9,500	
Stocks, Mutual Funds	13,100	3,400	9,700
Motorcycle	3,600	SOLD	3,600
Cash Value Life Insurance	5,300	SOLD	4,400 (after taxes)
Car 1	12,000	12,000	
Car 2	7,400	7,400	
	$192,700	**$171,600**	**$20,200**

LIABILITIES		Reduced To:	Amount Applied:
Mortgage	$102,000	$102,000	
Home Equity Loan	7,500	7,500	
Master Card	4,700	0	$4,700
Visa	3,800	0	3,800
Discover	2,400	0	2,400
JC Penney Card	1,900	0	1,900
Sears Card	1,200	0	1,200
Car Loan 1	6,200	0	6,200
Car Loan 2	2,300	2,300	
	$132,000	**$111,800**	**$20,200**

One thing that I would like to point out about this series of transactions is that they are basically "net-worth neutral." Although the Joneses' total assets have obviously declined, the debt has declined by a like amount. The resulting net worth of $59,800 ($171,600 in assets less $111,800 in debts) is very close to the original net worth of $60,700. The slight reduction is the result of having paid some income taxes on the cash-surrender value of the liquidated whole life policy. The most important result of this strategy, however, is the impact on the monthly cash flow. Let's take a look at the revised budget.

—Mike and Mary Joneses' Final Budget Revision—

CATEGORY	AMOUNT	RATE/NOTES
Mortgage	$1,160	8.50% (30-year; 26 years left)
		(with taxes and insurance)
Home Equity Loan	110	10.50% (15-year; 9 years left)
Car Loan #1	0	*Eliminated*
Car Loan #2	265	11.25% (3-year; 1 year left)
Master Card	0	*Eliminated*
Visa	0	*Eliminated*
Discover	0	*Eliminated*
JC Penney Card	0	*Eliminated*
Sears Card	0	*Eliminated*
Giving	200	
Saving	100	
Food	400	
Gas and Electric	175	
Telephone	70	
Cell Phone	30	
Life Insurance	45	
Auto Insurance	105	
Motorcycle Insurance	0	*Sold*
Gas and Oil	110	*Reduced due to motorcycle sale*
Cable TV	30	
Dining Out	100	
Gym Membership	0	
Lunches Out (Mike)	20	
Tennis Lessons (Mary)	0	
Babysitting	40	
Total Monthly Expenses:	**$2,960**	*Reduced by additional $561/month*
Mike's Net Income	2,925	After taxes, insurance
Mary's Net Income	740	After taxes
Total Monthly Income	**$3,665**	
Margin	705	*Improved from $144*

One important explanatory note concerns my recommendation to pay off the first car loan. One question that might arise is why I would suggest paying off the first car loan and not the second when the latter has both a higher monthly payment and higher interest rate. Another question is why, in light of our stated desire to free the maximum amount of monthly cash flow for debt repayment, did I recommend paying off the Discover card rather than the second car loan. The balances were nearly identical, and although Discover had a higher interest rate, the monthly payment was only $60 as opposed to the $265 car payment.

The answer to the first question involves the remaining term of the loan. Since we aren't planning to liquidate additional securities or savings to further reduce debt, I chose to keep the debt that would eliminate itself in the shortest period of time. Mike and Mary will get another significant boost to their monthly cash flow in twelve months when the second car loan is paid off. The answer to the second question is that, of all the loans that could have been repaid, the most attractive one to keep was the second car loan. The Discover card was very expensive and the low monthly payment was a negative, not a positive. If this had been the only way to immediately get to a positive cash flow I would have considered it. But we've already achieved a positive cash flow of $705 per month, and that is with the $265 per month car payment. Next year the positive cash flow will increase to nearly $1,000 per month when the remaining car loan is paid off.

The other important issue that might have escaped your notice involves the amount of the newly created positive cash flow. Does the figure $705 per month have any particular significance? If not, look back at the revised budget. You'll notice that this figure is almost identical to the amount of Mary's take-home pay. Do you remember which goal was her top priority? For the first time in years the Joneses can actually start talking about Mary's becoming a stay-at-home mom. They might not make this decision immediately because it would cause them to return to a tight monthly budget with no cash flow margin. They might plan, however, to have Mary stop working next year when the second car is paid off.

The Joneses will go through the process of looking through the attic and garage to see if they have anything else of value to sell. Mike will also look to increase his income in order to start rebuilding their savings. If cash flow allows, I'll also suggest they look into combining both mortgages and refinancing to a single, fifteen-year mortgage. This will save them a considerable amount of interest over the term of the loan and actually bring into focus the possibility of being completely debt free. More importantly, going through the five steps together has helped to eliminate virtually all of the financial tension and stress that was negatively impacting their marriage and family.

—Mike's Perspective—

As we discussed, Mike concluded in prayer that it was best to go ahead and sell the motorcycle, both to repay debt and to increase the time he spends with the family. He also realized that very few of his assets were likely to generate a higher return than he has been paying in interest on his debts. He didn't want to sell everything, but was willing to take a major step in that direction in order to move toward the immediate goal of eliminating all consumer debt.

—Mary's Perspective—

Mary had always liked the perceived security of having several bank accounts, an IRA, and investments, but she had felt strangled by the debt load. Mary is glad to trade some of the assets for an immediate reduction in debt, especially when she considers the impact it will have on further reducing their monthly expenses. She is very excited that Mike has decided, without any pressure from her, to sell his motorcycle.

—Compromise Objectives—

The resulting decisions are outlined in the final budget revision given previously. Because Mike and Mary were both active participants in the process, there was unity on all of the decisions. They have decided to sit down with the kids and try to explain the cause of the family tension that has existed recently, to ask for forgiveness for the impact on the kids, and to commit to moving forward as a team.

—Key Biblical Principles—

The wicked borrow and do not repay.

—Psalm 37:21

Give everyone what you owe him.... Let no debt remain outstanding, except the continuing debt to love one another.

—Romans 13:7-8

The rich rule over the poor, and the borrower is servant to the lender.

—Proverbs 22:7

And my God will meet all your needs according to his glorious riches in Christ Jesus.

—Philippians 4:19

Congratulations! You have invested a significant amount of your valuable time in learning what God's Word has to say about managing your finances. You have studied the biblical principles and have participated in a case study to help apply what you have learned. Regardless of your personal financial state, I pray that you have benefited in some way from this study. Once you've mastered these principles, I would encourage you to share them with others. We are surrounded by folks in financial crisis, and many would be willing to implement biblical financial principles if someone would show them how. You will be blessed as you share what God has taught you.

As for those of you who are struggling with finances and having difficulty managing the resources that God has entrusted to you, I implore you to implement the advice in this study. Let us heed the word of caution given us in James 1:22-25:

Do not merely listen to the word, and so deceive yourselves. Do what it says. Anyone who listens to the word but does not do what it says is like a man who looks at his face in a mirror and, after looking at himself, goes away and immediately forgets what he looks like. But the man who looks intently into the perfect law that gives freedom, and continues to do this, not forgetting what he has heard, but doing it – he will be blessed in what he does.

Study diligently God's plan for managing those resources that He has entrusted to you, and then endeavor to obey the principles so clearly laid out in His Word. As you do, prepare to be blessed. God is faithful, and He alone *is able to do immeasurably more than all we ask or imagine* (Ephesians 3:20). To Him be the glory!

STUDY QUESTIONS

1. What is the purpose of creating a list of assets and debts (a statement of net worth)?

_____

_____

_____

2. As assets are liquidated in order to repay debt, how should the order be determined in which to pay off various loans and credit cards?

_____

_____

_____

3. Why is it often worthwhile to liquidate stocks and mutual funds to repay credit-card debt?

_____

_____

_____

4. What is God's primary means of providing for our income needs?

_____

_____

_____

5. In what ways can an excessive debt load begin to impact our relationships with the Lord and with other people?

_____

_____

_____

6. What are some of the practical benefits of achieving financial freedom?

_____

_____

_____

-APPENDIX-
PERSONAL TESTIMONY

"For all have sinned and fall short of the glory of God....The wages [penalty] of sin is death."

—The Apostle Paul, Romans 3:23; 6:23

"For God so loved the world that he gave his one and only Son, that whoever believes in him shall not perish but have eternal life."

—The Apostle John, John 3:16

For some readers this will be the most significant chapter in this book. Financial freedom, as important as it is, pales in comparison to spiritual freedom. Many of us, especially those who have known the pain of financial mismanagement, have lived with the false assumption that solving their money problems will solve all other problems in their lives as well. Reality, however, begs to differ. Indeed, many folks who have managed their finances well and have accumulated sufficient resources to ensure financial independence, continue to struggle in other areas of their lives: lack of purpose or fulfillment, broken relationships, loneliness, guilt, or addictions. Money will never solve the various personal challenges that we face in our daily lives. One of the most profound questions that Jesus asked His followers goes right to the heart of this issue: *"What good will it be for a man if he gains the whole world, yet forfeits his soul?"* (Matthew 16:26).

The Problem

For most of my adult life, "gaining the whole world" sounded pretty good to me. I wanted desperately to succeed, and like many people, I defined success by two things: money and possessions. I had become convinced that financial success was the only sure means of achieving happiness, peace, and contentment. My goal was simple: to accumulate enough money to buy whatever I wanted, to live wherever I wanted, and to stop working whenever I wanted. In short, I wanted to be rich. To be sure, money was only a means to an end; it wasn't the money itself that I craved, but the happiness and contentment I was sure the money would bring.

Things started happening pretty quickly after I entered the financial industry in 1985. Almost immediately I started earning more money than ever before, and with it came the affluent lifestyle I always wanted. Every few years we would get a new house, new cars, new furniture. I never actually saved any money, choosing instead to spend everything I earned on a lavish lifestyle. I quickly learned that when you have a high income, the banks will line up to lend you whatever you need to buy whatever you want. The more I borrowed, the more they lent.

There was just one problem. As any of you who have struggled with materialism are well aware, when you're caught up in this cycle, it doesn't matter how badly you wanted something or how much you thought you would enjoy it, within a few weeks of your actually getting it the thrill always wears off. And when you are living a highly leveraged lifestyle, always borrowing in order to buy, the thrill usually wears off around the time that the payment book comes in the mail. Then you realize that, even though this new "toy" doesn't matter to you anymore, you're going to be paying for it for the next three, five, or ten years.

Everything came to a head when I finally convinced my wife that we should go ahead and build our dream home. It was a beautiful two-story colonial house on four wooded acres in northern Baltimore County. I promised my wife that if I could just build this house I would be happy, and we wouldn't ever have to move again. But the second Saturday in our new home, when Lori came to call me for breakfast, she found me sitting on the foyer staircase staring intently out the window, apparently with a troubled look on my face. When she asked me what I was thinking about, I explained that I had just set a new goal for our family. We were going to build an even bigger house. And instead of this measly four acres we were going to have ten. And horses…we would have enough property to get some horses. (I was sure that one would get her!)

When I could see that Lori wasn't buying into my new plan, I went into my lecture mode: "You have to keep setting goals. When you stop setting goals, you stagnate. Setting goals is why we have all this stuff and why we're so happy." She let me ramble on for five minutes or so, and then she looked at me with the saddest eyes and said, "Jim, when can we be done?"

She continued, "You don't have to do this for me; the kids and I were happy when we lived in the apartment with bugs in it. This stuff doesn't matter to us."

That, my friends, was the equivalent of a heavyweight boxer's uppercut to the midsection, because for the first time in my life I had to admit that this was all about me. It wasn't about trying to be a good husband and father, or about providing for my family. It was all about me: my ego, my pride, and my insatiable appetite for material things. Even worse, far from providing any sense of financial security for my family, I had actually brought us to the brink of financial ruin. The big house, new cars, built-in pool, and condo at the beach looked great from the outside, but I had actually constructed a lifestyle that required a monthly income of $10,000 just to pay the bills. And remember, I was in a commission business. There was no guaranteed income; every month I started at zero. Needless to say, work wasn't much fun anymore. For the first time in my life I realized that I was absolutely lost.

The Solution

Not too long after that one of my friends invited me to a businessmen's Bible study. He said that several guys with whom he played basketball had decided to meet once a week for this Bible study and I was welcome to join them. I can tell you that, had he asked me six months earlier, I probably would have laughed at him. But at this particular time in my life, I realized that I didn't have the answers. I only knew that my life had no meaning or purpose. My so-called success had led to a sense of increasing despair. That elusive sense of peace and contentment seemed to be drifting ever further away from my grasp. I didn't expect to find my sense of meaning and purpose by attending a Bible study, but I was open to anything that might help to make sense of my life.

The first few months of the study I didn't get very involved. Sometimes I understood what they were talking about, sometimes not. But one Monday morning we had an interesting experience when we arrived. The guy who led the study had been called out of town late Sunday night. There wasn't enough time for him to ask anyone to fill in, so when we got there, there was no one to lead the study. Instead, the group got into a fascinating discussion about the following question: If you only had a few minutes to explain to someone the *main message* in the Bible, what would you say?

There were two things I knew about the Bible: one, that it was very thick, and two, the print was extremely small. There wasn't much chance of my reading the whole Book on my own, but these guys were going to make it easy by giving me the abbreviated version. What was the main message of the Bible, the central theme that was so important to God to convey that He had it committed to writing all those years ago? I couldn't wait to hear the answer.

They started going around the table and everyone found out pretty quickly that it was hard to do this in just a few minutes. Several guys fumbled through it, until we finally got around to Doug. Doug was sitting on the edge of his seat, waiting for his turn. He was so excited he jumped up from his chair and ran to the front of the conference room. We had one of those big, white grease boards with dry erase markers, and Doug was going to give us a visual illustration of the main message of the Bible.

Up in the top left-hand corner of the board, in huge letters, he wrote the word *God*, G-O-D. Beneath that, he started to write several attributes, or characteristics, that God says are true about Himself. For example, he wrote the word *holy*, and mentioned a verse in the Bible where God says, *"Therefore be holy, because I am holy"* (Leviticus 11:45). Beneath the word *holy*, he wrote the word *perfect*. Then he quoted a verse in the Bible in which Jesus said, *"Be perfect, therefore, as your heavenly Father is perfect"* (Matthew 5:48). And beneath the word *perfect,* he wrote the word *judge.* He went on to explain that the Bible tells us that God is a judge, and that at some point He's coming back to judge the world.

On the other side of the board, in great big letters, he wrote the word *man*: M-A-N. Then he went on to tell us what God has to say about us — about me. The first thing he wrote beneath the word *man* was the word *sin*. He mentioned a verse from the Bible that says, *All have sinned and fall short of the glory of God* (Romans 3:23). I have to admit that I didn't particularly like being told that I had sinned, but neither did I have to think about it very long to realize that it was true. Beneath the word *sin* he wrote the word *death*. He mentioned a verse from the Bible that says, *For the wages of sin* – or the penalty for sin - *is death* (Romans 6:23). Doug went on to explain that the Bible wasn't just talking about physical death, which to me would be punishment enough, but spiritual death – eternal separation from God. In other words, hell.

I was starting to get a clear picture of the main message of the Bible. God was in heaven, perfectly holy, perfectly perfect, and preparing to come back and judge the world. Here I was on the other side, already declared guilty by God of sin, and already sentenced to death. Not only death in this life, but sentenced to hell for all eternity. I was squirming in my seat at this point, and finally Doug got around to the good part. In the middle of the board, between the words *God* and *man,* he drew a huge cross. The cross represented Jesus Christ, and Doug explained that Jesus came to earth to die in our place, to pay the penalty for our sin. He quoted a verse that says, *For God so loved the world* – that's us – *that he gave his one and only Son* – that's Jesus – *that whoever believes in him shall not perish but have eternal life* (John 3:16).

You see, God is perfectly just. The standard He sets for us is absolute moral perfection. Failure to live up to that standard is sin, and because God is just, sin must be punished. But God is also perfectly merciful. Because of our sin we can never earn our own way into heaven, so God provided a way for us by sacrificing His own Son to die in our place. When Jesus hung on the cross — beaten, bruised, and bloodied — it wasn't for His own sin that He was being punished; God makes it very clear that Jesus was without sin. Rather, He was being punished for our sins, yours and mine. And when God raised Him from the dead it was His way of showing us that Jesus' sacrifice was acceptable. Through Jesus, we can be made right with God, have our sins forgiven, and enjoy eternal life in heaven.

I was excited. I had never heard this before, and I remember wondering, *Well, what's my part?* I understood God's part, and I understood Jesus' part, but what did God want me to do about it? Doug closed with the answer: Simply believe. Our part is to take God at His Word and believe that what He says is true. He mentioned a verse that says, *If you confess with your mouth, "Jesus is Lord," and believe in your heart that God raised him from the dead, you will be saved* (Romans 10:9). Not "should be," "could be," or "might be." You *"will be"* saved. Friend, our part is to believe God, and to put our trust in Jesus Christ for the forgiveness of our sins and the promise of eternity in heaven.

As soon as I got in my car and headed back to the office, I fumbled through a prayer. I don't remember the exact words, but the essence of it was that I understood that I had sinned and could never earn my way into heaven. I understood that my penalty should have been eternal death, but that Jesus died in my place so that I could be forgiven. I believed God.

The Result

There have been many significant changes in my life since that day in the spring of 1992. I'll spare you the details of most of them, but I do want to share two changes in particular, because they were immediate and dramatic. The first has to do with how I viewed people. I used to be one of the most selfish people I knew. I viewed relationships only in terms of what I could get out of them. This wasn't always outwardly evident; I was much too clever to let my true colors show. But the fact was that I didn't care much about other people, especially people who were in need. I was one of those "positive-mental-attitude" guys, so if somebody had problems in their life they could just keep it away from me – I didn't want to be bothered with negatives.

But right after I became a Christian my heart started to change. I began to develop a genuine interest in other people, particularly those in need. I wanted to know what was going on in their lives and what challenges they were facing. If they were hurting, I wanted to help. So much so that, although my favorite thing to do with money had previously been to buy myself another toy, I began to start having more fun using my money to help those who were in need. I know this probably doesn't sound like a big deal to some of you because you have always been generous. But if you understand where I was coming from, and my attitude toward people and money, this was a dramatic change and it happened almost immediately.

The second change, and the most significant, was an overwhelming sense of happiness, peace, and contentment. Finally, my life had meaning and purpose. I came to understand that God has a plan for my life, and every day I'm watching that plan unfold. Most importantly, if I should die tonight, I know with absolute certainty where I'll spend eternity – in heaven with God. Not because I was one of the good guys; believe me, I wasn't and I'm still not. It's because I have taken God at His Word and believe that what He says is true. My hope for the forgiveness of my sins and for the promise of eternal life rests exclusively in the hands of Jesus Christ, my Savior and Lord.

Conclusion

It has been my prayer that God would use this Bible study, not only to lead many people to financial freedom, but to personal freedom as well; the former is pointless without the latter. Remember Jesus' words: *"What good will it be for a man if he gains the whole world, yet forfeits his soul?"* (Matthew 16:26). There is much more to this life than money, and money cannot purchase your eternal security. Jesus Christ has purchased it for you, taking upon Himself the punishment for your sins and demonstrating His perfect love for His people: *Greater love has no one than this, that he lay down his life for his friends* (John 15:13).

If you have never made the decision to believe God by placing your trust in Jesus Christ for the forgiveness of your sins and His promise of eternal life in heaven, it is my prayer that you will do so today. Experience the unconditional love and forgiveness that God alone can give, and be free from all guilt and shame. Accept this precious gift that He so freely gives, and enjoy the rich blessing of a life filled with meaning and purpose. And when this life is over, may we rejoice together in God's presence, secure in Him for all eternity.

> *Jesus answered, "I am the way and the truth and the life. No one comes to the Father except through me."*
>
> —John 14:6